Solitude
Stillness
Serenity

DENIS DUNCAN is a minister of the Church of Scotland, formerly editor of *British Weekly* and Director of the Churches' Council for Health and Healing. He was also Associate Director and Training Supervisor at Westminster Pastoral Foundation, Director of Highgate Counselling Centre, and of Hampstead Counselling Service, all in London. Earlier he served in St Margaret's Parish in Juniper Green, Edinburgh and Trinity / Duke Street Parish, Glasgow.

The focus of his current ministry is 'Proclamation through preaching, print and publishing.'

ALSO BY DENIS DUNCAN

A Day at a Time
Creative Silence
Health and Healing: A Ministry to Wholeness
Love, the Word that Heals
Here is my Hand

BOOKS EDITED BY DENIS DUNCAN

Through the Year with William Barclay
Every Day with William Barclay
Marching Orders
Marching On
Through the Year with J. B. Phillips
Through the Year with Cardinal Heenan

75 Saturday Meditations from
𝕿𝖍𝖊 𝕯𝖆𝖎𝖑𝖞 𝕿𝖊𝖑𝖊𝖌𝖗𝖆𝖕𝖍

Solitude
Stillness
Serenity

by

Denis Duncan

ARTHUR JAMES
BERKHAMSTED

First published in Great Britain in 1997 by

ARTHUR JAMES LTD
70 Cross Oak Road
Berkhamsted
Hertfordshire HP4 3HZ

ISBN 0 85305 368 5

Typeset in Monotype Plantin Light by
Strathmore Publishing Services, London N7

Printed and bound in Great Britain by
Guernsey Press Ltd, Guernsey, CI

I dedicate this second book of Meditations –
as I did the first, *Be Still and Know...* –
to my wife, Ettie, who died on 16 October 1993, and who
was for 51 years my partner on the way.

As she also served on the staff of the *Daily Telegraph*
for over twenty years, particularly as secretary
to Max Hastings, then Editor-in-Chief,
it is the more appropriate that these volumes of
Saturday Meditations from that paper
should be dedicated to her.

Contents

Part III: In the World

Part IV: Times and Seasons

A Meditation for Lent

Foreword

We live in a culture which has reduced the spiritual to the psychological. That could even be the definition of the secular. At the same time, not many people would care to put their whole trust in psychology, as their ancestors placed their trust in God. As a result, we have become an orphan people, with nowhere to turn when we must turn somewhere.

Yet help is available under our very noses. It is not necessary to journey to the ashrams of India, or delve into the exotic mysteries of Zen or Yoga, in order to discover our spiritual roots. The Christian tradition lays all its riches before us, if we could only recognise them for what they are. But often we need a guide; and those with the necessary skills are few.

One guide with these gifts in abundance is Denis Duncan. This book gathers together in one place many of his articles which have been published in *The Daily Telegraph* under the heading 'Meditations'. For some of his readers this will be a reunion with old friends. Dr Duncan is a writer whose columns are cut out and kept, often to grow dog-eared within the folds of a wallet or purse. Such readers will find, to their pleasure, that in this case the total is even greater than the sum of its parts.

For other readers this will be a first introduction. It will be a rewarding encounter, not only for Christians but for those of any religion or none. Good spiritual writing transcends denominations, and can readily cross the boundaries between faiths. The ability to speak to people of all sorts and conditions is a sure test of true spirituality. That mysterious thing we exchange when we love and are loved, here on earth, is not a different thing from the love of God, of which the spiritual writer writes. To better understand the one is to better understand the other. And they are the entrance to the understanding of suffering, when love turns to pain.

What denies us access to the ancient and modern wisdom of Christianity is our own ignorance or fear, or that over-familiarity which breeds contempt or indifference – or maybe, most of all, the hidden but pernicious influence of cultural fashion. Embarrassment at being thought 'religious' may be a poor reason for turning away from the only thing that is likely to help us, but in the present age it is a common reason nevertheless.

In the sensitive hands of Denis Duncan, the Christian faith becomes much more than a collection of texts or doc-trines, and the Christian life something much deeper than a habit of church-going. It becomes an exploration and spir-itual journey. 'Through prayer, meditation and contempla-tion our level of spiritual awareness can change too ...' he writes at one point. And later he explains 'It is open to all who humbly seek and reverently ask, to be allowed ... to touch and handle things unseen'. There is a sense of beckoning on, a leading forth, in his writing which puts me in mind of some of the metaphysical poetry of George Herbert. Above all, neither of them makes religion 'difficult' in a technical or intellectual way. Denis Duncan addresses people in their ordinary conditions and takes them as they are. I believe he also moves them on. It is a rare and extraordinary gift.

CLIFFORD LONGLEY
May 1994

Note: This Foreword was generously contributed to the first volume of these meditations, published as *Be Still and Know....* The Foreword is, with Mr Longley's cordial agreement, reprinted here as a further seventy-five meditations are published under the title *Solitude, Stillness, Serenity.* His gracious comments on the first one hundred meditations apply, I hope, to the next seventy-five. – D.D.

Introduction

It has been my privilege and pleasure to contribute Saturday Meditations to *The Daily Telegraph* regularly since 1990. These have normally appeared in 13-week series, twice a year, with another contributor writing the intervening series. *Be Still and Know...* contained one hundred of these Meditations. *Silence, Solitude, Serenity* brings together another seventy-five of them.

It is a matter for gratitude that a paper of national and international standing, with a circulation of well over one million copies daily, continues to include a religious meditation in its Saturday edition. That edition reaches an even wider circulation than on weekdays. I do not suggest for one moment that the Meditation is of interest to, or read by, all those millions of readers of the paper, but the volume of correspondence I receive indicates something of the value placed on the contributions. Letters come from members of all denominations, from readers both clerical and lay, from people on the fringe of faith, from Jewish readers and, at times, from those who are not religious at all.

Writing is an important medium of communication for me and represents an essential part of my commitment to 'proclamation through preaching, print and publishing'. I therefore value the opportunity this ministry provides.

Writing 500 words is much more difficult than producing 2,000! The restriction is nevertheless a valuable exercise in discipline. Every word must count. Deviations and digressions cannot be entertained. The necessarily limited space allocated to the Meditation must be respected, as must that demanding factor deadlines (long-familiar to me as Editor for thirteen years of *British Weekly,* the national religious newspaper. But these pressures combine to compel the completion of the Meditation on time and to enforce the necessary 'tightness' in writing so necessary in journalism.

The awareness I have of the scope and variety of the readership of *The Daily Telegraph* also influences my approach. The Meditations will be read by clergy looking for some profundity of concept, academics used to an intellectual approach, lay people seeking inspiration and, possibly most of all, all kinds of individual people who long for pastoral support with spiritual insight. It is important to have empathy with *their* situation, which may well be one of profound suffering and inner pain. The Meditation must speak of the things that are eternal, but also convince the reader that I am aware of the harsh, temporal realities with which people have to cope.

Writing these as I do, not in long-planned series but simply responding to week-by-week needs, events and situations, there is inevitably repetition of references and phrases. To these, where it is desirable, I have drawn attention. I feel however that the Meditations should appear just as they did over the years. There are therefore references to contemporary events, but they were written at that time and can, I feel, remain. Occasionally headings have been slightly adjusted as, over the years, one or two were too similar.

When my greatly beloved and honoured predecessor in this ministry, the late Bishop George Appleton, was asked by the then Editor of *The Daily Telegraph*, William (now Lord) Deedes to undertake this task, he was told that his function was to expound 'the eternal verities', that is, the great religious truths and realities. I have made that my guideline too, and so my Meditations aim to be just that, a reflecting on the great spiritual foundations of the faith. I hope I have succeeded in doing this with profound simplicity – that is, writing of deep things in understandable language. If through these Meditations someone has been encouraged, inspired, comforted or sustained, then their purpose is met.

In quoting from the Psalms, I have used the numbering in the Authorised Version of the Bible. I have made frequent use too of William Barclay's translation of the New Testament.

Just as I expressed in 1994 my gratitude to Max Hastings, then Editor-in-Chief of *The Daily Telegraph* for his asking me to write these Meditations, so now I offer similar appreciation to his successor in the editorial chair, Charles Moore, for continuing that commission. The Foreword, contributed by Clifford Longley, the distinguished journalist, for *Be Still and Know...* has been reproduced here with his kind permission. I am grateful to the secretaries and input staff of *The Daily Telegraph* who deal so helpfully with my copy, and to the marketing staff of Telegraph Books who handle the Telegraph sales of both books, and of the audio cassette of *Be Still and Know...*, which is also a Telegraph Books production.

To have been allowed to effect this ministry in print in such a great national newspaper is, I repeat, an immense privilege. To have the Meditations reaching yet further out into the world is a happy but humbling thought. Fifty of these are, incidentally, now available on a three-hour audio cassette which I recorded under the title *Be Still and Know...*. It is available from Telegraph Books (1 Canada Square, Canary Wharf, London E14 5DT). I hope someone, somewhere, will find both books and cassette a blessing.

DENIS DUNCAN
February 1997

The Bliss of Solitude

'I want to be alone,' drawled the late Greta Garbo, the statement becoming a catchphrase for ever associated with that famous screen actress. It cannot have been a longing for loneliness. It must have been a plea for privacy.

To be alone means two different things. On one hand it describes a state which none can enjoy, some dread, and many experience. How awful is that utter loneliness which belongs, in John Betjeman's phrase, to 'the poor, unbeloved ones' – their lot in this world. But the same phrase can refer to solitude, as positive a concept as loneliness is a negative one. The latter is enforced, the former chosen. One brings pain, the other peace.

The cry of the lonely for family, friends, fellowship is heart-rending. Bereft of living contact, they become resentful and bitter. Lost in an unloving world, they deserve our pity. Sadly it sometimes happens that, devoid of other relationships, they find the church too has let them down. Some survive, coping without complaint and accepting their aloneness with resignation. Others, inwardly angry over their experience of life, condemn themselves to isolation and project their problems on an uncaring world.

Solitude is totally different. It is something to be sought as creative and beneficial. The reasons for seeking it may not always be healthy. For some, increasing dependence on retreat becomes nothing more than a running away from the world and its problems. For others however, solitude is sought for profound religious reasons at the heart of which is the need to be alone with God and, in God's presence, with ourselves. 'How sweet, how passing sweet is solitude,' wrote William Cowper. It was something which he, with his inner turbulence, needed as much as any other. There is no experience more profound or valuable than being alone, in proper solitude.

The record of Jesus's life makes clear his need for withdrawal to the quiet place. He had to get away from the demanding crowds who waited for his teaching and yearned for his healing. He made solitude a habit. If it is a New Testament precept that 'the disciple must be as the master', it is a precept all too difficult to fulfil. His thoughts and our thoughts, his ways and our ways, are far from each other. But the obligation remains. 'Try to have the same attitude to life that Jesus had,' Paul wrote to the Philippians. Like him, we need to practise as Wordsworth calls it 'the bliss of solitude'. It is only in the desert place and alone that we can discern the will of God.

The saints know it. Those with a profoundly simple faith know it.

True religion begins with a confession of faith and develops in a commitment for life. Spiritual growth is of the essence of that commitment, which demands both devotion and discipline. A key factor in that process must surely be the practice of solitude.

A Time for Stillness

Jesus was a Jew, steeped in the wonder of his 'bible', our Old Testament. His spirituality was shaped, humanly speaking, by the glory of the Law and the witness of the prophets. From such sources there came the bases of his thinking, the inspiration of his teaching, the depths of his ideas and the stimuli for his imagination. He was, naturally, very much aware of the deep longing of his people for the coming of the Messiah, the deliverer of his people. That hope lasted for a long period. Even at the time of his ascension, there were those among his disciples who were asking: 'Will you now restore the kingdom to Israel?'

Following the divine affirmation given at his baptism by John in the Jordan, Jesus wrestled with the meaning of his calling. Through forty days and forty nights, he struggled with the temptations implicit in his call to be Messiah. There was much in the Old Testament that painted the accepted picture of the Messiah as a warrior king, a concept he ultimately had to reject. He found the image of the Messiah as a suffering servant in that same Old Testament, a concept that expressed what he felt about his calling. A moving, dramatic figure, the Suffering Servant would be despised and rejected by men and women, a figure of sorrow and acquainted with grief. When he entered Jerusalem in triumph, Jesus came not as the warrior king on a charger, but in humility, on an ass.

What a treasure-house of spirituality the Old Testament is! It provided for Jesus – as it did for Judaism, as it does for the Christian faith – a source-book of inspiration, a course-book on faith. And how important it was in relation to the

Incarnation. It was the book that documented the on-going revelation of God to people. Jesus came 'in the fulness of the time', a phrase which sums up that combination of history and geography which made Palestine the place in which he must be born. He came as a Jew because Judaism was spiritually so developed, so advanced in its understanding of the eternal dimension, so aware of its relationship to God that it had to be the cradle of the Incarnation.

The Old Testament is a book which has much war, violence and strife in it, but it is also the book that testifies to the value of stillness. Turn for example to Psalm 23 with its still waters, green pastures and the capacity to restore the soul; to Psalm 46 with its counsel to 'Be still and know that I am God'; to the story of Elijah, under pressure from the prophets of Baal, being advised to heed not earthquakes, wind and fire, but only 'a still, small voice'. It was surely from the Old Testament that Jesus learned the supreme importance of stillness in the devotional life.

If life today is to be tolerable and productive, it is essential to learn the meaning of stillness. We need a time not for talking but for listening; that time for total concentration on, and contemplation of, God.

Serenity

If time is given to solitude, and attention is given in the stillness, then spiritual growth will reveal itself in greater inner peace and serenity. As a result, the ability to cope with the vicissitudes of life will be truly strengthened.

One of the occasions when Jesus deliberately sought solitude followed the feeding of the five thousand people. The disciples were sent on their way back across the Sea of Galilee. Jesus found stillness in his quiet place, but the disciples were experiencing turmoil on the water. As sometimes happened on that lake, a storm of considerable ferocity blew up, creating alarm for the followers of the Lord. It was in that crisis that Jesus appeared, walking on the water, strengthened by his time of solitude and stillness. With the authority he alone could command, he calmed the waves, stilled the storm and soothed the fearful disciples with his presence. 'It is a spirit,' they cried. 'It is I,' he said. 'Be not afraid.' The serenity of their Lord, and the authority he proclaimed, left them in wonder and admiration. As they said on another occasion, 'Why, even the wind and waves obey him'.

Jesus showed that same impressive serenity in his response to his accusers and to those who blasphemed against him. Tested, tried, taunted, he simply 'answered them nothing'. He managed to maintain serenity too under the harshest of provocation, when in Gethsemane he faced the ultimate test. It seemed, momentarily, that he wavered: 'Father, let this cup pass from me,' he cried – but immediately recovered that still, serene centre as, in trust, he prayed: 'Nevertheless, not my will but thine be done'.

The power of the church lies in the strength of its individuals. It needs for its corporate witness the spiritual power of its members. If the 'spiritual blaze', of which Alexander Solzhenitsyn speaks as essential at the watershed of history marked by the millennium, is to be created it will come from the spiritual commitment and drive of individual people.★

When pupils reach the day of leaving at the Rudolf Steiner school in which they have learned the meaning and importance of the wholeness of life and the essential place of the spiritual in that wholeness, they are allowed to share in a traditional custom. It is a moving ceremony, only for those who are leaving. Wisely, the school feels there is gain in keeping some experiences back in a world too much given to introducing young people to every experience too soon. Clothed in white gowns, and with burning torches in their hands, the departing pupils make their way in a line to a field beyond the school where a huge bonfire is standing, unlit. They form a circle round the pile and then, at a given moment, all plunge their flaming brands into the bonfire and a colossal blaze leaps up to illuminate the countryside for miles. And round that blaze, songs are sung.

Those who can best contribute to the spiritual blaze we need are those who, coming from the solitude and the stillness, reflect the serenity of Christ.

★ See fuller reference in *A Spiritual Blaze*, Number 32.

Part I

Quiet Time

The Divine Patience

How privileged were Peter, James and John to share in two great moments – one glorious, one dark – in Jesus's life! One was his transfiguration, the other his agony in the Garden of Gethsemane. Peter's excitement at the mountain top vision of Moses and Elijah, as well as the sight of Jesus embraced in radiant light, was manifest and understandable. Less easy to comprehend was the inability of the three disciples to remain awake while Jesus agonised in Gethsemane over his coming suffering and death. How sad his words sound: 'Could you not watch with me one hour?' They could not, and so did not see the sweat 'like drops of blood' that indicated the tension he was experiencing in that strife of prayer.

That searching phrase, 'the strife of prayer', comes from Jacques Loew, the Dominican monk who pioneered the worker-priest movement in France. In his book *Face to Face with God** he pinpoints the prime 'characteristics of all prayer and all struggle: patience, perseverance and constancy'. The element of patience is a crucial one.

'Though God take the sun out of heaven,' wrote George Herbert, 'we must have patience.' Paul certainly counselled Timothy to 'follow after patience' and in the second letter of Peter it is strongly emphasised as a virtue.

It is, however, its association with suffering (both words come from the same Latin root) which is significant. Patience is, in fact, writes Robert Llewelyn, 'that quality of life which makes suffering creative'. How appropriate it is then to reflect on patience, for the sacrifice of Jesus, and his understanding of it in terms of the great Old Testament concept of 'the suffering Servant', incarnate the compassion of a God of love 'who suffers long and is kind'.

The divine patience is a prominent biblical theme. Of many references to it, the most glorious description comes surely from the Psalmist: 'Thou, Lord, art a God, full of compassion, and gracious, long-suffering and plenteous in mercy ...' (Psalm 86). The Greek word for 'long-suffering' is *makrothumia*. It is the word used by Paul to tell the Romans of the goodness, forbearance and long-suffering of God. It is the attitude personified by the waiting father, ready to receive his prodigal son, not with anger or judgement, but with heart-felt love. That picture encapsulates Jesus's portrayal of the patient God.

The church, in its proclamation of the gospel, must surely present not the God of wrath but the God of compassion, whose love, in the words of the benediction, 'passeth understanding'. Redemptive love unites patience and passion.

If the religious life is an attempt to reflect divine qualities and attributes, George Herbert is right: 'We must have patience'. In so doing, we mirror in some small way the divine patience, our example and our joy.

---

* Darton, Longman and Todd (1977).

Love's Extravagance

Jesus, probably to our great surprise and certainly that of the disciples who witnessed the event, once commended sheer extravagance! It is worth reflecting on that act of love, both graciously received and highly commended, an example of love's proper extravagance.

The story is well known. It is told, with differing details, in several Gospels, but the essence of the occasion is agreed by all. While Jesus was dining, a woman anointed Jesus's feet with a very 'costly' and 'precious' ointment and wiped them with her hair. It was the sincerity of that loving act that moved Jesus to say, in answer to 'indignant' comments from the disciples about waste, that this story of extravagant love would be retold wherever the gospel was preached. That indicates Jesus's valuation of the gesture.

The word 'extravagance' comes from two Latin roots meaning to 'wander beyond' the limits of the normal and the expected. It then takes on pejorative connotations – excess, immoderation, unnecessary lavishness and even (the disciples' word) waste. 'Why was this ointment not sold for three hundred pence and given to the poor?' asks Judas Iscariot. Jesus did not question the need to minister to the poor; the gospel is concerned with the weak, whatever the reasons for their weakness. But poverty, he comments, is a perpetual problem. There will always be the need – and the opportunity to deal with it. What the woman had done was so special as to be unique, and that needed to be realised. The woman herself could not possibly see the gesture in the symbolic way that Jesus did – as a reference to his death and burial; for her, it was an offering of grateful love to someone she admired. Those with much to be forgiven (maybe she was in that category) want to give much. There is a time for love to be extravagant.

When, in Stainer's *Crucifixion*, the moving words 'God so loved the world' are proclaimed, there is a notable emphasis on the word *so*, for it is the word that puts on record that God went 'beyond the bounds' to ensure that 'whosoever believeth in him should not perish but have everlasting life'. It is that little word *so* which dramatically emphasises the extravagance of the divine love, forgiveness and compassion.

'Jesus, thy boundless love to me no thought can reach, no tongue declare.' So runs John Wesley's translation of Gerhardt's hymn. The only response can be unconditional love to God and 'our neighbour'. But there are those who may feel that they have, in personal relationships, loved too much. The result has been rejection, betrayal, denial, pain. But can we ever love too much? Love such as this woman gave to Jesus is *never* wasted.

To love and not to count the cost can be a permissible and proper extravagance. It has its roots in the Incarnation which is indeed the extravagance of God.

Serene Stability

To know *about* God is one thing. To know God is another. Theology, once described as 'the queen of the sciences', is an intellectual necessity and an invaluable discipline. May there always be those qualified and equipped to pursue it. It is not, however, the most important element in healthy religion. Religion is focussed on and embedded in relationship and, primarily, the relationship between God and humankind. It is in relationship that God reveals the essence of the divine love.

The wonder of worship is not confined to the intellectual element essential in its celebration, though that element is always present (we are to love God with our *minds* as well as our other faculties). It is rather a positive response to the One who, we are told by St John, 'first loved us'. It is a consequence of the divine initiative in that primary relationship that all other relationships are mandatory – love towards others, towards the earth from which we come, and to ourselves. From these relationships come the disciplines of pastoral care, ecological concern and that most important of pastoral attitudes, the need to accept ourselves 'as we are'. It is on that basis that God accepts us. What is equally important is that loving our neighbour 'as ourselves' depends on a humble but loving self-acceptance.

Worship encapsulates that complex of relationships and roots it in *coming* to praise and *going* to serve. Jesus's invitation to the 'weary and heavy-laden' to *come* and find rest and refreshment relates paradoxically to his command to '*go* into all the world' in mission and service. Liturgy is that relationship and its derivatives expressed in prayers of adoration, thanksgiving, confession and absolution, and of intercession. Mysticism is a being in touch with God in non-verbal but profound experiences of the divine presence. Indeed 'true mysticism', writes Wyons Mauleverer, is most intimately concerned with 'loving contact with him in whom we believe ... we find our rest in Him'.

Finding such rest in relationship takes us back to that great statement in the *Confessions* of St Augustine: 'Thou hast made us for Thyself and our hearts are restless till they rest in Thee'. Restlessness is essentially a negative spiritual condition, whether it be in Augustine's north Africa in the fourth century or here and now in the uneasy dis-ease of the late twentieth century. It is the church's function in an uncertain world to encourage men and women to 'find God' and experience the relationship of love through which there is the possibility of stability today and serenity tomorrow.

'Oh that I knew where I might find Him' is the heartfelt cry from Job. The mystic who wrote *The Cloud of Unknowing* points to the answer. It is related to the opening sentences of this meditation: 'By love may He be gotten and holden, but by thought never'.

God is infinitely far away yet, paradoxically, very near: 'Closer is He than breathing and nearer than hands or feet'. Worship is the acting out of that sense of relationship with God and with each other, with ourselves and with the earth.

Silence and Simplicity

The more real the underlying unity of the church, the more it can tolerate variety – and even afford to encourage it. Genuine movement towards unity should not be felt as threatening to distinctive witness but rather as an opportunity to integrate into the evolving corpus of belief and practice valuable historic insights into the faith.

It has been a privilege and benefit to me that two-thirds of my ministry has been in ecumenical undertakings. The blessings of such wider sharing do not change my primary calling which is to be committed to the ministry of Word and Sacraments, a task I see to be of primary importance today, but my ministry has been enhanced indeed through my interdenominational experience.

To take something from another tradition and add it to one's own, if it is valid both biblically and theologically, does not deny or abnegate one's faith, just as making an effort to *understand* other faiths does not conflict with one's own 'Christ-centredness'.

There may however remain areas of spirituality that still lie largely outside our experience. One of these may be disciplined and, particularly, contemplative prayer. Contemplative prayer and its related lifestyle has four elements. These are, as Thomas Keating (Cistercian priest, monk, abbot) records:* Solitude, Silence, Simplicity, and a Discipline for Prayer and Action. That four-fold definition is in itself ancient.

* *An Invitation to Love* (published by Element).

It is manifestly easier to carry out these practices in the controlled (organisationally) ambience of the convent, the monastery or the community but working out these elements of spirituality in our personal daily life remains a highly desirable aim.

The cultivation of the benefits of *solitude* is a strength in the struggle against unconscious motivation, that process (all too familiar to St Paul) whereby negative inner pressures, coming from depths outside the reach of our memories, overrule our conscious desires for good. Father Keating, while holding that 'the language of psychology is an essential vehicle in our time to explain the healing of the unconscious', goes so far as to say that 'only the passive purifications of contemplative prayer can effect this profound healing. Only then will the reservoir of interior silence, built up in periods of contemplative prayer, never run dry.' That statement will not necessarily be accepted in all psychotherapeutic circles but it deserves deep reflection.

Simplicity of faith can be a strength, too. It is not an attitude of simplistic naïveté that skates superficially over the great problems of life. It is a clear-sighted vision, a spiritual understanding, not necessarily able to be put into theological terms or philosophical argument, that has been vouchsafed to the earnest seeker, educated or less educated, articulate or inarticulate.

A young woman I have known for many years wrote to me to say that so hectic was her life – work, family, etc. – that, in her spiritual life, 'God is getting the short straws'. A dedicated woman, committed to service of great value, she reminds us, as she reminds herself, that to keep the spiritual balance right, we do need that fourth element, a discipline for prayer and action.

Finding Peace

Those who follow Jesus want to take him at his word. After all, it was said of him that, unlike others, he spoke with authority. But trying to be obedient to his words can bring severe problems to some people. He said, for example, 'If you ask any thing in my name, I will do it'. There are sincere people who have become bitter when the 'any thing' for which they pleaded 'in his name' was not given.

What then did Jesus mean when he said: 'Take no anxious thought for tomorrow'? Given the realities of life today, how do you do that? When cuts in jobs are predicted and family responsibilities are great, can you be other than anxious about the future? When paedophile rings threaten the safety of the children, is it not a worry? Insurance companies prosper just because of anxiety about the future: is it not prudent to prepare for risks over property and life? The loss of a partner will bring not only loneliness, but worry about tomorrow. When temptation persists and inner pressures compel the repetition of abhorred sins, guilt can bring overwhelming anxiety. An anxious world teems with anxious people. Advice that seems over-simplistic cannot meet such deep needs.

'How blessed is he who leads a country life, unvex'd with anxious cares,' wrote the poet John Dryden. Perhaps in the simpler world of Palestine, in Jesus's time, it was easier to 'consider the lilies of the field, how they grow', and contemplate 'the fowls of the air', fed by 'your heavenly Father'. It is less easy to take no anxious thought for tomorrow in the relentlessly demanding, often depressing, actively threatening world that is ours today.

The importance of Jesus's exhortation surely lies not in a literal interpretation of his words but rather in a recognition of the principle which he expounds. Anxiety is unprofitable and unhealthily negative. Just as fear casts out love, so worry destroys inner peace. Concentrating on illnesses only encourages ill-health. Even in prayer it is not good to focus on problems rather than God. It is love which casts out fear. Giving out does us much more good than giving in. We cannot, by an act of will, banish anxiety. We can reduce its pressure by reflecting deeply on 'the things which we most surely believe'.

There is so much to encourage us in the doctrine of Providence, its wonders seen through the eye of faith. The glory of the doctrine of forgiveness is its capacity to demolish persistent anxiety over guilt. Salvation is not a merit to be earned. It is a gift of grace, and anxiety is eased thereby. To believe in the healing Christ is to know God's will for us is wholeness. And if there is anxiety as to where energy can come from, remember that first Pentecost when promised power filled the disciples.

There is indeed encouragement in the contemplation of the 'deep roots and firm foundations' of our faith.

Spiritual Growth

'Well! My poor heart, here we are, fallen into the ditch which we had made so firm a resolution to avoid; let us implore the mercy of God, and trust that He will help us to be more steadfast in future....'

These words from the great mystic, Francis de Sales, will touch a nerve in us if we are honest people. It is the story of the spiritual life as it has been experienced by seekers throughout the ages. Julian of Norwich expounds the same theme. In the parable of the Servant who 'hurried off so hopefully to do his Lord's will' she writes: 'And anon he falleth into a slade and taketh full hurt'. St Paul certainly knew the experience Francis de Sales describes. 'The good that I would, I do not,' he told the Roman Christians, 'but the evil that I would not, that I do.'

The vocabulary of religion describes this experience as 'temptation'. The language of psychotherapy will think of it as negative pressures coming from the 'shadow' side of the unconscious. The effect is the same. There is nothing more discouraging in the development of the spiritual life than the persistent sense of failure in thought and, even worse, behaviour when self-discipline falters, and faults believed to have been overcome are repeated. For the alcoholic, dedicated to overcome his or her 'problem', but who falls again, the sense of despair can be devastating. Someone struggling against sexual temptation experienced as intense inner pressures, not always understood, can be made nearly suicidal by another 'failure'. What is even worse is the fact that such moments of weakness may follow times of heightened spiritual activity when the sense of grace is strong. How vulnerable we can be at such times!

Such falling into the ditch or slade must not however lead to a persistent dwelling on, and analysis of, failure. Brother Lawrence, in *The Practice of the Presence of God,* offers spiritual common-sense for our comfort and encouragement. He was much 'aware of his sins but was not discouraged by them; he confessed them to God and did not ask Him to excuse them. When he had done so he returned in peace to his ordinary business of love and worship.' Add 'she' to 'he' each time, and we have practical spiritual direction of great value for us all.

It is in the same spirit that Francis de Sales offers his prescription for temptation in the quotation with which I began:

'Here we are, fallen into a ditch': *admit it.*
'Let us implore the mercy of God': *confess it.*
'Trust that He will help us': *have faith.*
'God shall help us': *leave it, forgiven.*

'Two are better than one,' said the Preacher (Ecclesiastes), 'for if they fall then one will lift up his fellow.' The battle for spiritual progress can be carried on privately with the help of God, but it is also the very purpose of spiritual direction and/or pastoral counselling to provide support on the spiritual journey. Sharing and caring is a God-given way to forward spiritual growth. Use it!

The Pain of Growth

It was Sunday morning. The hymn, enthusiastically sung, was 'The Church's one foundation'. A line in a verse not printed in all hymnaries had a searing impact. 'The cry goes up "How long?"' Saturated as we are by images of suffering, it seemed to express the anguish so prevalent today. The context – the line relates to disunity in the church – was temporarily overlaid by mental pictures of the hurt, harried, homeless people in, for example, Bosnia, leaving loved ones behind to their fate. The cry does indeed go up: 'How long, Lord? How long?' Will the suffering of the world and such people never end? Can it at least be diminished?

To offer, unasked, religious platitudes to those overwhelmed by human tragedy is spiritual insensitivity of an indefensible kind. How can the simplistic text be relevant to, or 'heard' by, the husband who has just lost his young wife to cancer? to the survivor whose loved ones have been killed in the accident? to the parents of the child who has died through 'natural causes', cot death, murder, suicide? It will, therefore, probably be with anger that the following words are read:

> The person who truly wishes to be healed is the one who does not refuse treatment. This treatment consists of the pain and distress brought on by various misfortunes. He who refuses it does not realise what they accomplish for him in this world or what he will gain when he departs this life.

The language is dated – this statement was in fact made a

very long time ago by St Maximus the Confessor. It was made the focal point in a talk given by a friend, an Anglican priest, when addressing colleagues on 'Healing through Dying'. His purpose was to bring some hope in relation to the problem of suffering, and to do it not in terms of doctrinaire, academic theology, but through the theology of experience.

Saxon Walker's wife, Sheila, knew for a year that she was dying of cancer but, as Saxon tells us in his book *Sheila – a Healing through Dying*,* that year was to be for them both the most spiritually creative year of their lives. They deliberately and consciously lived out the Christian Year, with its painful parts and its glorious parts, discovering as they did so such growth, healing and wholeness that Sheila's last year became not a failure but a victory, not a death but a new life.

The same principle, the creative power of pain, was something that had to be firmly put to the many applicants I had to interview over their desire to be trained in a psychotherapeutic model of counselling. The pain of growth had to be faced. My German colleague in Frankfurt, Dr Werner Becher, a psychotherapist, told me: 'If you ever want to experience hell, undertake analysis.' The statement may be exaggerated but it makes its point. The road to (in Jung's word) 'individuation' or wholeness runs through the vale of tears.

In the spiritual life, the way to sanctification also involves the pain of spiritual growth. If, in St Maximus's word, the 'treatment' is resisted, maturity is postponed. It can never lightly be claimed that suffering has an inherently creative component, but it is always true that the journey from the despair of the Garden of Eden to the wonder of the Garden of the Resurrection passes through the Garden of Gethsemane.

* Published by Arthur James.

The Joy of Growth

When I had the responsibility for selecting potential trainees for a training in counselling on an analytic model, I was always impressed by the fact that a very high percentage of these 'mature' applicants were people who had themselves experienced counselling or psychotherapy as 'clients'. In other words, having themselves gone through problems and experienced the pain of growth in doing so, they wanted now to help others find the joy of growth too.

Whatever our undertakings in life, it is almost always necessary to endure pain to achieve success. Behind the musician, gloriously interpreting music in song or with an instrument, there lie hours of practice, scales, arpeggios, exercises, discipline. The ecstasy in performance is worth the agony of preparation. For athletes who are to perform at the Olympic Games there are the long routines essential to build up muscles, sinews, stamina. For footballers seriously injured, there may be years of painful recovery programmes before the joy of public performance is possible again. The Formula One driver faces discomfort, danger and death to have the joy of knocking part of a second off his lap-time. Across the whole field of human endeavour – what pain there is in preparation! What joy in achievement!

Growth into maturity psychologically and/or spiritually, reflects the same process. Blocks have to be cleared. Knots have to be unravelled. Defences have to come down, perhaps a little, probably a lot. Creative growth depends on the pain of self-awareness and self-discovery and, in this process, the first steps may be the most demanding ones.

St Paul speaks of present suffering and future glory when he exclaims: 'I reckon that the sufferings of this present time are not worthy to be compared with the glory that shall be revealed in us!' As with a woman in childbirth, the pain is now, the joy is to come. When the Psalmist proclaims that 'God has put a new song in my mouth', he is testifying to the joy of growth. Zacchaeus, an unhappy man, guilty of shady practices, ostracised by the people because was a tax-gatherer, shows the inner pain that made him climb up a sycamore tree to see Jesus, who might help him. To read his story is to feel his pain. To hear his declaration of recompense and reconciliation is to sense his incipient joy. The process is a glorious one.

'All through my life I have been aware of the power of God, guiding me,' writes Lin Berwick,* cerebral palsied, blind and in a wheelchair, in her book *Inner Vision*,† 'displaying all too clearly how He wants me to use the dark, as well as the joyful, periods. Adversity can be changed to joy so long as we accept the will of God.'

'Weeping may endure for a night, but joy cometh in the morning.'

Worship should reflect the joy of growth. Rightly and properly worship includes the essential element of confession, but the ultimate purpose of all worship is uplift and encouragement. For at the heart of it is praise and thanksgiving for His promise of the miracle which can bring newness of life and the joy of growth.

---

* See Number 33, 'Rejoice and Sign!', for more about Lin.
† Available only from The Lin Berwick Trust, 9 Hunter Drive, Hornchurch, Essex RM12 5TP (tel: 01708 477582).

Spiritual Energy

What to say and do to bring about changes of mood is the challenge that faces preachers, pastors, spiritual directors, psychotherapists, counsellors and politicians. 'Mood,' in dictionary terms, is 'a contemporary state of the emotions'. Additionally, it means 'a prevailing spirit, disposition or set of attitudes'. The first definition takes mood out of the realm of rational control. The second points to the problems that arise for politicians.

Much evidence is offered by politicians to show that the recession is over and economic growth is at hand. There is, however, a major difference between that public presentation and the actual mood of ordinary people. Daily experience in small businesses involves worry about survival, jobs, homes and families. Confidence in the future is unsteady and statistics, on their own, just do not take away the mood of despondency.

The Irish situation illustrates the same dilemma. Assurances about the cessation of violence are just not strong enough to meet the deeply ingrained lack of trust in some people – as the debate about the word 'permanent' in relation to a cease-fire has shown. It will need more reassurance than has so far been given to remove doubt from the collective unconscious of some groups. Indeed, something of a conversion experience may be necessary to close the gap between public pronouncement and private misgiving.

In the religious field, conversion needs to be as thorough as anywhere else. Jesus pointed to the dangers of superficial religious experience in the parable of the sower. Seed that cannot root properly because there is no depth will endure for some time but ultimately fade away. Pastors and preachers need to be aware that, unless conversion reaches the unconscious level, it will not hold. Indeed, the transformation required is effectively re-birth, Jesus said to Nicodemus. Bringing about the 'new creation' of which Paul speaks involves radical and total change. Only then will attitudes, relationships and behaviour be affected.

Moods are a problem in our personal lives too. We can suddenly find ourselves 'spiralling downwards' into gloom and depression, and not understand why it is happening. Perhaps some event has acted as a trigger and activated feelings of rejection, lack of worth or bereavement. Other causes may be unconscious and beyond our reach. We cannot simply will ourselves out of that dark mood but, hopefully, we can find help in two directions. If some new factor enters the situation (the dreaded interview was in fact highly successful, for example), a dramatic change in mood is possible. Our other lifeline may be the love of a friend or the expertise of a counsellor. Most people need company to be strong enough to look at and then face the factors that pull us down.

We also need to draw on the resources of our faith. There is, or ought to be, in our religion, access to the spiritual energy that can lead us away from decline into depression and disease, and take us towards health and wholeness. Historic Christianity calls that energy the Holy Spirit who, at Pentecost, so dramatically changed the mood of the disciples.

True Greatness

It is not often that you feel that you are in the presence of true greatness; greatness, that is, in the New Testament sense of the word. I experienced that feeling acutely when, many years ago, I was introduced to a physically insignificant but spiritually colossal man, famous for his work for the poor and deprived in the slums of Kobe in Japan. He was, of course, Toyohiko Kagawa. Himself racked by ill-health, he had fired the spirit in so many of us in our younger days. 'Lives of great men all remind us,' wrote Longfellow, 'that we can make our lives sublime. And, departing, leave behind us Footprints on the sands of time'. How powerful is the influence of the truly great!

There was an occasion when Jesus's disciples disputed among themselves as to who should be the greatest. Jesus answered by placing a child amongst them. 'It is the one who thinks as little of his importance as this little child,' he said, 'who is the greatest in the kingdom of heaven.' The greatest are those who, like Kagawa, are least conscious of being great.

In Paul's letter to the Philippians, there is a profound theological statement about the Incarnation. It encapsulates the wonder of the humility of God. Paul writes: 'Christ Jesus ... did not regard his equality with God as a thing to be clutched to himself but ... took upon himself the form of a servant. He humbled himself and became obedient unto death, even death on a cross.' Here is a statement about the true greatness of Jesus stated in glorious terms! The corollary is specific: 'Let this mind be in you which was also in Christ Jesus,' he says. True greatness involves true humility in us all.

Reflecting on the theme of greatness, I cannot but refer to the lamented death of Rabbi Hugo Gryn. I was in his presence only once, but the sense of his greatness was borne in upon me. Others have now made it clear how great he was. 'Men like him happen only once in a lifetime,' wrote two of his friends. 'We are fortunate it happened in ours.'

The breadth and depth of Hugo Gryn's outlook was so much part of his stature. 'He was a born ecumenist,' said the writer of his obituary in this newspaper*, 'a man who spent his professional career searching for common ground between all faiths.' To do that was not a denial of his Jewish faith, just as it is not a denial of Christ-centred Christianity to sense glimpses of the truth in many places. Indeed, the firmer the convictions of the Christian, the more there is confidence in genuine exploration. J. B. Phillips was so right. We must not make our God too small.

Encounter with true greatness is always life-enhancing – as I felt after my meeting with Kagawa. Be moved deeply then by what others wrote of Hugo Gryn: 'We are a group of Asians, Blacks and Jews who were inspired by Hugo Gryn to laugh together, grow fond of each other and air our harmonising views as he did, forcibly and regularly.'

It is only the truly great who enable others to leave such footprints.

* *The Daily Telegraph.*

Holy Simplicity

'We may be giants scientifically,' said a contributor to a recent BBC Moral Maze programme, 'but morally we are pygmies.' That statement points to the discrepancy between the sophistication of scientific, technological and (thankfully) medical progress and our ability to cope with the moral and spiritual questions posited by such developments. Its basic validity should not however lead us, as it does some religious people, to dismiss contemporary life as wholly amoral or immoral, and modern people as increasingly corrupt. That is the injustice of over-generalisation. Despite the terrible crimes committed, especially against children; despite the rampant materialism in so much thinking and the unhealthy sensuality that provides so much news; despite the awfulness of persistent wars, the violence, rape and murders, the drug traffic, and the madness of irresponsible people with guns, what is wonderful about God's world is the amount of goodness shown by so many people, the high degree of moral awareness reflected at many levels and the glorious spirituality of humble, anonymous folk. It is right to recognise the deficiencies in moral and spiritual life today. It is not right to see the world and its people as beyond redemption.

That said, it is necessary to recognise how easily we can be corrupted. Greed, for example, is highly infectious. We can all become 'locked in' to contemporary materialism and the economic struggle to survive. The problem for all religious people is how to remain 'untarnished by the world'; how to fulfil the injunction 'not to be conformed to this world' but to be 'transformed'. Just here is a crucial point of witness for disciples.

In creating a 'manual for Christians' today, four areas of current failure need attention. *Rule 1* concerns *the simple life*: the reference is the reminder that 'the Son of Man had nowhere to lay his head'. *Rule 2* deals with *priorities*: the reference here is to Jesus's instruction to 'seek first the Kingdom and its righteousness and all these (other) things will be added to you'. *Rule 3* lays down the importance of *perspective*: the reference is to the stance laid down by St Paul, 'the things which are seen are temporal but the things which are not seen are eternal'. *Rule 4* deals with the importance of *direction*: the reference is to the biblical exhortation to run the race of life, 'looking unto Jesus'.

However impossible is the achievement of it, it is important to hold on to the ideal of the simple life, to retain what Ben Jonson calls 'the grace of simplicity'. 'Teach us delight in simple things,' we sing in Rudyard Kipling's hymn. It is not wrong to be modern, to have and to enjoy the things that are part of life today, but it is good for the soul to keep alive the sense of simplicity. 'Cultivate simplicity,' wrote Charles Lamb to Samuel Taylor Coleridge. But perhaps simplicity alone is not enough. 'I have always revered *holy simplicity*,' said St Jerome. Those who have tried to get back to the way of the Lord have usually done so by seeking to reflect Jesus's simple life and practising holy simplicity. '*O sancta simplicitas!*' cried John Huss, as he died. 'O holy simplicity!'

Conflict and Comfort

It was that true saint, George Johnstone Jeffrey, who insisted that every sermon must conclude with a message of comfort. William Barclay spoke similarly about worship. 'Every act of worship,' he wrote, 'must include the note of comfort.' With that, all will surely agree. But there is a problem. The Gospel does not only bring comfort. It brings conflict.

That that is true is made clear in a saying of Jesus recorded in Matthew's Gospel: 'Think not that I am come to send peace on earth; I came not to send peace, but a sword.' He offers an explanation of this dramatic statement: 'For I am come to set a man at variance against his father, and the daughter against her mother.... And a man's foes shall be they of his own household.' Conflict indeed!

The point in this passage is the nature of commitment. 'He that loveth father or mother more than me is not worthy of me,' Jesus says. It is a daunting declaration. But is it a statement about intention, or rather about consequences? Loyalty to Christ can, as a matter of fact, bring extreme conflict to families. William Barclay's translation of the passage confirms this: 'You must not suppose that the result of my coming will be peace for the world. The result of my coming will not be peace, but a sword. My coming is bound to result in a cleavage between a man and his father, between a daughter and her mother....' Loyalty such as Christ demands can and does cause conflict. If comfort and conflict are associated with the gospel, should not every act of worship take account of both of them?

The role of the prophet, certainly in the Old Testament,

44

includes the need to be a nuisance – to authority and those in whom authority is vested, to powers-that-be, both public and ecclesiastical. 'Is that you, you troubler of Israel?' King Ahab asks the prophet Elijah, who replies that it is his duty to trouble not Israel, but Ahab and his house because of their wickedness. The modern preacher is not exempt from the prophet's responsibility, that is the need to subject policies and programmes to the scrutiny of God's will and declare God's judgement on them without fear or favour, especially if they harm people, endanger the social fabric or seek the interest not of all but of the few. The result of such denunciation may well be conflict.

Preaching is, however, but one element in a service, so William Barclay's dictum about worship needs to be fulfilled. Those who go from church must do so with a sense of comfort in both the sense of inner serenity and of spiritual encouragement.

'Comforter, where is your comforting?' asks Gerard Manley Hopkins as he agonisingly reflects on that tragedy of which 'no worse, there is none'. To provide comfort is of the essence of the gospel and every act of worship must represent the compassion of the Lord.

It takes skill and sensitivity to hold together, in one act of worship, the possibility of conflict and the necessity of comfort. Perhaps the key to achieving it is always to 'speak the truth in love'.

Part II

The Spiritual Journey

Travelling On

I was moved by the frail, elderly lady who spoke to me after the service on Sunday. 'I could not hear you,' she said, 'because I am deaf. Nor could I see you because I am nearly blind. But how I sensed the spirit in the atmosphere!'

My dictionary defines religion as 'belief in, recognition of, or an awakened sense of a higher, unseen controlling power or powers....' It was to this sense of the numinous, the inner consciousness of another dimension, that this lady surely testified. It is something experienced through what Paul describes as the 'knowledge which is beyond knowledge'. It relates to the reality of 'the things which are eternal'. This world is, alas, deeply affected by materialism, conditioned by public relations, market forces, political, economic and social pressures. All canvass the value of wealth and possessions. Sadly, such pressures relentlessly force those who cannot cope with such demands towards poverty and repossessions. How essential it is then to proclaim to such a world – and this is a primary task of the churches – the need for the recognition of the dimension within which Jesus lived and on which the early church was founded, the dimension of the Spirit.

When John Baillie entitled one of his books *Invitation to Pilgrimage,* he pointed to the nature of the journey of faith. We are, says William Wordsworth, 'travellers between life and death', travelling on to our spiritual destiny. It means taking risks even to the extent of being thought 'fools for Christ's sake'. But it is an exhilarating process involving purpose, direction and movement. This pilgrimage is never easy. There will be peaks of spiritual experience and deep troughs of despondency and despair. 'My marks and sores I carry with me', said Mr Valiant-for-Truth in John Bunyan's *The Pilgrim's Progress*, 'to be a witness for me that I have fought his battles.' Whether our pilgrimage be seen as a race (as Paul saw it) or a struggling plod, it is a journey of destiny and excitement so long as we 'keep looking unto Jesus'.

The pilgrim goes where the Spirit leads. It is a journey made in freedom, with spiritual growth and increased inner awareness the symptoms of forward movement. How beautifully the dove, the image of the Holy Spirit, symbolises both movement and freedom! The Genesis picture, too, is of the Spirit *moving* upon the face of the waters, while both Testaments speak of the Spirit in terms of wind and breath, elements invisible and unable to be grasped, but energising and free-flowing. That Spirit must not be quenched or contained by hidebound dogma, ecclesiastical regulations, spiritual censorship or the privatisation of belief. Like the wind, the Spirit 'blows where it wills'. And if freedom has its risks, the word of God is always that against which we test our experience.

Perhaps, in the end, Wordsworth's claim that we are all 'travellers between life and death' needs emendation. We are, in fact, travellers from death to Life.

True Worship

'Let us worship God,' I said on Sunday morning as I called the congregation to praise and prayer. I must have used these words around three thousand times in my years of ministry. But therein lies a danger. The sheer familiarity of the words may make us unaware of the problems people feel over religious terms taken for granted. 'Worship' is a difficult word for some people.

The point was brought home to me by a business executive who read a Meditation in which I described worship as an acting-out of the relationship of love which is at the heart of faith. In a gracious and thoughtful letter (he is by profession 'an ideas and implementation planner'), he writes: 'I find it impossible to build such a word (worship) into any meaningful relationship between man and God if that relationship is built on a relationship of love. Even if one accepts the (in my view) wholly misleading metaphor of Father in place of God, I still find worship an impossible ingredient in that relationship. Did you worship your father, or encourage your children to worship you?'

The word 'worship' creates different images. I am sure it is our interpretation of the word itself that causes difficulty. 'O come, let us worship and bow down' cried the Psalmist. 'Let us kneel before the Lord our maker, for he is our God....' As with so many Old Testament images and metaphors drawn from contemporary ideas and institutions, worship appears to involve two levels: monarch and subjects, 'almighty' God and his servants, omnipotence and powerlessness. This encounter between divine authority and human weakness certainly feels inappropriate to a relationship of love. But such a form of relationship on two levels is, in fact, encouraged by the Hebrew word used eighty-six times in the Old Testament to translate 'worship'. It means 'to prostrate oneself'. Perhaps the difficulty over the word 'worship' relates to the associations it has with an emphasis on the divine sovereignty. Are such attitudes what we expect people to feel in response to the call 'Let us worship God'?

It is better to look in another direction and that is to the Anglo-Saxon root of the word; worship is derived from *weorthscipe* which means 'honour'. Recognition of worth prompts respect, reverence, admiration, even love, and it is those words which point to the essence of worship. To worship God is to honour God and that leads us happily to Alan Richardson's definition of the purpose of worship: 'to offer praise to God for His grace and glory'. How appropriate this is to the relationship of love and familial bond.

How we honour God 'for his grace and glory' is a matter of tradition, temperament, choice and style. What is all-important is that worship reflects the best that we can offer – liturgically, musically, intellectually and spiritually.

'God is a Spirit,' said Jesus to the Samaritan woman. 'They that worship him must worship him in spirit and in truth'. Whatever we offer in worship must represent our utmost for the highest.

Treasure-store

The Bible is, by any standards, an extraordinary book. It is of immense literary value, abounding in both memorable poetry and abiding prose. It is a documentary concerned with human relationships and divine encounters. It recounts profound prophetic activity, solid social history and marvellous mythology (in the technical sense of that word). It is a book respected and admired by many, irrespective of religious adherence. It contains the wonder of the Old Testament scriptures and the glory of the New Testament Gospels. It provides, in the form of letters to Christian communities, incisive theology and deep pastoral concern and care. It enshrines, for the perpetual record, the history of the life and teaching of Jesus Christ. For many, it is 'the supreme rule of faith and life, the inspired authority, the Word of God'. What a wonderful book the Bible is!

All who love the Bible in its entirety will, nevertheless, have favourite parts. Those who value the Psalms and mark in red memorable phrases or verses will draw comfort, inspiration and devotional power from a true manual of the spiritual life. Who is not moved by the twenty-third psalm, with its green pastures, still waters and restoration of soul? A favourite prophet – and it might well be Ezekiel – will provide passages pulsating with spiritual stimulation and profound pastoral care. Those who appreciate St Paul (and there are those who don't!) will differ over his greatest contribution, but is it not remarkable that one and the same man can write a manual of theology such as his letter to the Romans is, and at the same time produce the glorious analysis of love in his first letter to the Corinthians, or his striking spiritual insight into the humility of Jesus in Philippians? And at the heart of the New Testament lie the three Synoptic Gospels which provide the essence of the record of Jesus – his teaching, preaching and healing, his encounters and relations, the flesh and blood Christ, the man of Nazareth, the prophet from Galilee, the Messiah as he saw himself, who came unto his own who 'received him not' – and St John proclaiming the cosmic Christ, the incarnate Christ, the crucified Christ, the risen Christ, the Christ who makes his continuing and abiding presence felt through 'another Comforter', the Holy Spirit.

'If I could have the privilege,' writes E. V. Rieu (in *The Four Gospels*) 'of a few moments talk with the four evangelists, I must confess that it would be St Luke whom I would confront with the longest set of questions.' Many would perhaps share that view, and for several reasons. For me there would be one area above all others on which I would want to hear St Luke, and that is on Jesus's healing ministry. For it is a doctor who records and reports on the healing miracles. That gives an authenticity and an authority to those 'signs of the Kingdom' of a very special kind. How glorious it would be to hear from a doctor's lips informed testimony to the reality and validity of those miracles in a way that only a physician could do it.

Called to Preach

'To everything there is a season,' declares The Preacher (Ecclesiastes). That applies, though he does not mention it, to 'a time to retire'. Churches now tend to lay down the age at which this must happen (partly for financial reasons). Such a trend is resisted by some and welcomed by many.

The concept of retirement from ministry does however give me a problem. The reason is stated dramatically by St Paul: 'Woe is me,' he cries 'if I preach not the gospel!' I empathise with that. *Called* to the ministry by God, and convinced of the imperative of preaching, how can I stop expounding the word?

The circumstances of my own call to the ministry may explain the strength of this feeling. The son of a clergyman, I spent my early years (apart from absence at boarding school) in manses. To the implicitly rhetorical question 'Will you follow in your father's footsteps?' I always offered a vehemently negative reply. I turned rather towards taking degrees in law at Edinburgh University. Poring one day over the *Institutes* of Justinian, suddenly and without forethought, I closed the book, returned it to the librarian, went home and announced that I would enter the ministry. Such an (as it was) irrational decision had serious lifelong implications for myself and my family, not least the abandonment of a potentially lucrative career in law for the stringent economics of the parish. I was convinced, however, that this was a divine call to service and could not be resisted. Many years on, I hold that view still. As a result, commitment to preach the gospel, in speech or written word, feels so mandatory that it cannot lightly be laid aside.

Such experiences of calling, as of conversion, are not always as instant as they seem. Paul's Damascus road experience demonstrates this. While the peak point in that story is the 'hysterical' collapse which he suffered under the bright light, it seems clear (with hindsight) that the one who was 'breathing out threatenings and slaughter against the disciples' was suffering inner conflict, touched off perhaps by the murder of the martyr, Stephen, to which he had consented. The conversion process had been under way, under the Spirit, for some time. It continued in his need to find the help of Ananias as his spiritual director. Now God's 'chosen vessel', he was called to lifelong discipleship. It is something of that compulsion that creates the preacher.

It is not generally fashionable today to present preaching as the primary means of communication, but increasingly there is an awareness of the need for its return to that position. The spiritual needs of today require the exposition of the word, a positive biblical theology, an informed pastoral sense grounded in love, a recognition of the healing gifts of the Spirit and the authority of personal spiritual experience. It is the function of the ministry to bring these blessings to the world.

'How shall they hear without a preacher?' So Paul writes to the Romans. Preaching is the priority in making known the gospel to the world. What a privilege those have who are called to preach!

The Glory of Life

'Do you know Bosshardt?' It is the question I always want to ask anyone from Holland – as I did when a guest of friends in Vienna. The young man's answer was typical. 'Everybody knows Bosshardt,' he said.

In earlier Meditations I have referred, in passing, to Major Alida Bosshardt.* Now *Colonel* Bosshardt (but always referred to publicly simply by her surname), she is officially retired, having given her life's ministry to serving those caught up in the sordid environment of Amsterdam's Red Light district.

She knew by name virtually every prostitute in the area. She was known to, and respected by, the owners of every pub and club, however unpleasant. She was loved by 'the girls'. She was never refused entry to *any* establishment to sell *War Cry*. A Salvation Army officer and evangelist, she was also a social worker. She believed a Salvationist should be professional in both disciplines. Profound and articulate when lecturing on her theology, she saw it expressed best in the simpler form of the poster on her living-room-cum-office-cum-study-cum-chapel. It reads:

The Glory of Life is to give, not get:
to serve, not be served;
to be a strong hand in the dark
to another in time of need;
to be a strength in a crisis of weakness.
This is to know the glory of life.

* I referred to Colonel Bosshardt in *Be Still and Know...* Numbers 31 and 80.

When I was reflecting on the word 'enthusiasm', it was Bosshardt who came leaping into my mind. Although that word is sometimes used in the secondary sense of emotional over-exuberance, it means (by derivation) 'possessed of God'. Bosshardt is, indeed, the enthusiast!

'Quench not the Spirit!' Paul wrote to the Thessalonians. To 'restrain' (*Good News Bible*) or 'suppress' (*The Jerusalem Bible*) the Holy Spirit, the source of true enthusiasm is, in William Barclay's rendering, 'to try to stop the activity of God', whether in oneself or in others. To be sure that we do not stifle the Spirit in ourselves demands self-examination and self-discipline. To destroy genuine spiritual enthusiasm in others – whether by discouraging their vision, denigrating the style of their ministries, or opposing every proposed change – is a sin not always absent from religious circles.

As we walked back to the Goodwill Centre in OZ Voorburgwal in Amsterdam, I heard her say to two of 'the girls' we met: 'This is the Scottish preacher who is writing a book about me.'* They approached me, hands outstretched. 'You won't do the Major any harm, will you?' one of them said. 'We love her.' That I could not do, for in Bosshardt I had found true spiritual enthusiasm, the Spirit unquenched.

'Sometimes I can point to success,' writes Bosshardt, 'for people have changed; men and women and children to whom you mean something. You do what you must do. You try hard. You care for all your co-workers. The result? It is God who does the book-keeping.'

Such ministry is indeed the glory of life.

---

* Published in 1977 as *Here is my hand!* (Hodder & Stoughton), but long out of print.

A Theology for Today

'There is not and cannot be a *new* theology. There can only be a re-occupying of positions which had once been taken up and subsequently abandoned or forgotten.' It was Alan Richardson, theologian and writer, who made that comment when he was referring to R. J. Campbell, minister early in this century at London's City Temple. Campbell was very much the focus of new ideas at the time and, in fact in 1907, wrote a book entitled *The New Theology*. The phrase has been used too of more recent endeavours to work out a relevant contemporary theology as the search goes on for ways to 'conceptualise' God.

Today's preachers can find themselves facing a practical problem of communication, one which arises from the different ways in which people think of God. In any typical congregation there will be many, probably the majority, who are at ease with traditional descriptions of God such as 'the Almighty' or 'the Father' and with the familial language related to that latter concept. They are happy to express their faith, prayers and doctrinal beliefs in a vocabulary drawn from scripture, and often from words used by Jesus himself. Any threat to that loved and revered language will be resisted.

Congregations today, in my experience, also include those who feel that traditional concepts of God are irrelevant or limiting. Intellectually unacceptable, they are a barrier to faith. Having come of theological age and anxious to 'put away childish things', they set aside as unhelpful images drawn from the regal and military models that are exclusively male. They deeply desire concepts and images that are 'meaningful' to them, that do not intellectually offend them and that are wider and therefore more embracing than they feel traditional terms to be. Perhaps to think of God as, in Paul Tillich's phrase, 'the ground of our being' is much more comfortable for them with its emphasis on immanence rather than on the transcendent God 'out there'. Others have moved on from that phrase to newer models and images.

When the preacher proclaims the Word, he or she stands not in a theoretical or academic context but in a pastoral one. Be the worshippers traditional or radical Christians, all have much in common. Whatever intellectual differences and difficulties are represented among them, all believe in God, all bring some kind of faith, all are seeking the religious life in some form, all are sinners (for The Good Book says: 'There is none righteous, no, not one ... for all have sinned and come short of the glory of God'), and *all need grace*. The offer of a right relationship with God, made possible by Jesus and sustained by the Holy Spirit, is there for all. 'How shall they hear without a preacher?' asks Paul. The preacher's task is not to wallow in theological intricacies but to meet spiritual needs, personal and corporate.

'God cannot be expressed, only addressed,' wrote Martin Buber in his seminal book, *I and Thou*. Wherever we are intellectually or devotionally, we all surely say in our need 'Abba, Father'. Faith is ultimately a relationship, however we try to explain it, with a personal God whose nature is love. This remains a theology for today.

Days of Doubt

'I'm struggling,' said the voice on the phone, four hundred miles away. It was Mary.* I had known her since she was fourteen years old, watched her through her formative years and conducted her wedding to John* thirty-nine years ago. Two months ago, when Mary rang me early in the morning, I had to assume it was bad news. It was. John had died from a heart attack during the night. Mary had faced the bereavement and funeral with courage, faith and dignity, but two months on, the depth of the loss was being felt. She was indeed 'struggling'.

When death comes suddenly, preventing long suffering, it must be a blessing to the one who has died, but it brings wounding hurt to those left behind. But how much worse is 'dying by inches'.

A devout Christian, for whom I have unreserved respect, used that phrase recently. She was referring not to the slow deterioration which is a normal part of ageing, but to her own experience of terrible suffering. Crippling deafness had brought her specialised ministry to young people to an end – and her to personal isolation. Surgical mismanagement had led to severe restrictions on mobility and appalling pain. Her ability to serve had been continually reduced. Dying by inches, with its combination of physical and spiritual agony, must test the faith of even the most committed saint. What can the will of God be in such a situation?

'Days of darkness still may meet me, sorrow's path I oft

* For privacy reasons, the names have been changed.

may tread,' says F. H. Rowley's hymn. He goes on: 'But his presence still is with me, by his guiding hand I'm led.' But, in days of doubt, can this feel real?

When sweat 'like drops of blood' fell from Jesus in Gethsemane, it was his day of doubt. He prayed that he might be spared the agony, but was able to add: 'Thy will, not mine, be done'. But the doubt seems to have remained: 'My God, my God, why hast thou forsaken me?' he cried from the cross.

It would be insensitive and arrogant for one unacquainted with such suffering to tell others to make the ultimate commitment and 'surrender all to Jesus'. How can one theorise on the spiritual benefits of 'detachment' or advocate in such circumstances 'catharsis', the spiritual process whereby an individual is 'cleansed or freed from such impediments – sensible, intellectual or spiritual – which block the quest for authentic existence and union with God' (Professor J. D. Jones)? How can one tell people to accept positively the darkness which is both the condition and the quality of the true knowledge of God (Denys the Areopagite)? Much more likely than 'surrender' is our taking to ourselves King Agrippa's word. 'Almost thou persuadest me....' Yet the weight of the counsel from the saints is that light comes out of darkness.

The darkest part of the night is the 'night of spirit'. St John of the Cross declares that that is 'the dark night of the soul' in which the self is stripped of any remaining spiritual gratification and of every consoling image of itself. Only beyond this, he says, does the dawn of illumination break into the final union.

It is a daunting, demanding journey, but the end of it is consolation, not desolation. It is, perhaps, 'growing by inches'.

Coping with Change

What incredible changes have taken place in my lifetime! As I look back to life in the Scottish village where I started school, I am amazed by its simplicity. We had no electric light or gas, only oil lamps. Ours was the first house in the village to have a 'wireless'. The large draughty Overland car my parents owned required strenuous cranking to start it.

It was a way of life unbelievably far from the world we know today with its scientific and technological wonders, jet-age travel, space exploration, laser beams. The degree of change, development and so-called progress has been phenomenal.

There have been other revolutions too: the medical world is an example. The tuberculosis that sent a considerable number of people from my Glasgow church of the 1950s to sanatoria and Switzerland is, now, virtually a thing of the past (but cancer is now the unconquered scourge). For the benefits of that medical revolution we must be grateful.

The sexual revolution is as real but more controversial. Attitudes to marriage, divorce and personal relationships have changed dramatically. Some will welcome what they see as greater honesty and openness in relationships today. Others will feel ill at ease with these developments.

How have we coped with such a process of change? Can we cope with it unless there has been significant spiritual development too?

I cannot demonstrate it but feel instinctively that corporately, socially, nationally, even ecclesiastically, spiritual awareness, sensitivity and power have declined over recent years. That does not mean that all is negative. There are many people of grace and goodness among us today, the equal of those in any other generation. There is also a spiritual searching in many, a feature more marked in the later years of my ministry. Crowded retreat houses and busy spiritual directors testify to that welcome situation.

Nevertheless the overall impression remains. So steeped is our world in materialism and secularism that spiritual receptiveness has been dimmed and the real presence of the spiritual factor in decision-taking and policy-making has been diminished.

When, in the Old Testament, the sense of the numinous declined or disappeared, the prophetic call was to repentance. The New Testament effectively opens with the same demand: 'Repent for the kingdom of heaven is at hand!' cried John the Baptist to the faithless. If ours is a world spiritually bereft and in need, then renewal is a priority for both world and church. But the church can lead the way in renewal only if it is itself willing to be renewed.

It is the prophet Ezekiel's vision of the miracle of resurrection in the valley of dry bones that, though it comes from another age, perhaps best points to the basic elements required to bring about renewal. They are the sense of the presence and power of God, the need to found faith on the Word and the awareness of the power of the Spirit as the agent in revival. These eternal verities are relevant for renewal today.

The New Creation

The disciples whose names are most familiar to many are, ironically, best known for their failures. Everyone is aware of Judas Iscariot and his betrayal of Jesus, as most would know Peter's denial of him. Thomas is associated with doubt, while James and his brother John publicly requested the most prestigious places when Jesus would come in his kingdom. The answer to this arrogance was, 'You know not what you ask'.

Peter, a great human being, had of course his successes too. So impressed was Jesus with Peter's confession of faith at Caesarea Philippi, that he said he would build his church on it; while Peter's spirit was willing, however, his flesh was weak. In the hour of crisis, Peter's instinct for self-preservation took over and the three-fold denial, foretold by Jesus, must have hurt. It is wounding to be publicly denied by those who love you. Peter knew that too. He wept bitterly.

Judas remains 'one of the most enigmatic figures of the New Testament', wrote Professor Thomas Kepler. It seems unlikely that his motivation was money, more that it was some aspect of power. Trusted as treasurer of the group, and part of the intimate circle, he had the opportunity possibly to force Jesus's hand in the national interest or perhaps to betray him for his refusal to denounce their Roman overlords. That Judas did not foresee the result of his actions led him to remorse and suicide.

Thomas's doubt is to his credit, not discredit. A pragmatic man, he was also patently honest. If his disbelief was a failing, Jesus did not criticise him for it, but he did commend those who believed in his resurrection without visible proof.

James and John, asking Jesus to do for them whatever they wanted and looking for prime places in the pecking order of the kingdom, demonstrated a total failure to understand their Master's aims. They provide a cautionary tale. Neither length of service nor progress on the ecclesiastical ladder guarantees an understanding of 'the things that are eternal'.

From this analysis of failure, destructive themes emerge – greed, power, selfishness, arrogance, lack of faith. But the weakness of these disciples is our weakness today, individually and corporately. We too seem bent on destruction. The power-seekers choose war to gain territory. Speculators and financial entrepreneurs profit at the expense of ordinary people. Those who insist on further nuclear tests endanger the earth (as, for example, Jacques Cousteau, the distinguished marine expert, has made clear), even when experts say there is no military or scientific reason to have them. The loveliness of sea and land is defiled by oil pollution and the supposed needs of travel and speed. Newspaper magnates glorify the trivial and peddle the pornography which often masquerade as education. What deprivation and degradation are the result of the destructive instincts of human beings! Yet men and women were intended not to destroy but to share in creation.

'In the beginning God created the heavens and the earth' and God has never ceased to create, as miracles, signs and wonders show. To be co-operators with God in creativity is the divine purpose. Humanity working together with God in a relationship of love is the only sure way to the new creation.

Unknown Disciples

If you advise someone unfamiliar with the New Testament to read it from beginning to end, it may be helpful to suggest that they start, not with Matthew's Gospel, but with Mark's. Not only is that one of the sources on which both Matthew and Luke drew but it will save the uninitiated from an immediate confrontation with Matthew's daunting list of names, linked together by repeated 'begats'. Those interested in Joseph's family tree, and indeed Israel's history, will find that genealogy valuable; early in my ministry I found it important for other reasons, and took my text for one Sunday morning from it. The particular phrase I selected is in verse three and reads: 'And Phares begat Esrom'.

I could, of course, have taken other people from that long list and made the same point for I knew nothing of Phares and Esrom but their names. Truth to tell, there is not much more to know. And that precisely is the point. *It is their anonymity which is important.* How contrary is this to the current emphasis on 'cult' figures, 'personalities' and 'celebrities' who, in popular press circles, are deemed to be so newsworthy. It is a shallow, superficial world that so glamorises the trivial. Those who make the biggest contribution to the things that matter most, such as creative living and unselfish loving, are often anonymous. Christianity certainly, and other religions equally, have reason to be grateful for their good, unknown disciples.

In many of our meditations, because of awful events, there has been constantly before us that most profound of problems, human suffering. Here I take a lighter theme which some may feel to be of no great significance or theological importance. It is, however, neither simplistic nor superficial, for it relates to the privilege of being used by God for long-term purposes, the end results of which we cannot ever know.

Phares and Esrom were essential links in the chain which stretches backwards to Abraham and forward to (as Matthew puts it) 'Joseph, the husband of Mary of whom was born Jesus, who is called Christ'. In other words, they were – although they could not know it this side of heaven – participants in the process that culminated in the Incarnation. A privilege, indeed.

Unknown disciples are unlikely to feature in the headlines. In the field of human suffering, however, they are the people who often minister to the devastated, the disturbed, the poor, the aged, the terminally ill, the battered, the bereaved, the broken-hearted. The pages of religious history are gloriously illuminated by the goodness of unknown disciples, whose characteristics are love and anonymity.

When Christians come together to celebrate Holy Communion, they will remember, as they must, the One who is the focal point of the sacrament: 'This do in remembrance of me'. Perhaps too they should not forget those unknown and unnamed people who, with love and care, laid the table and provided the bread and wine for the Last Supper, for they too shared anonymously in helping to make known the whole gospel to the whole world.

Distractions from Discipleship

There is a danger that public introspection in church circles over personal relationships, combined with confusing ecclesiastical messages in relation to sexual morality, could blunt the authority of the church in matters spiritual. The media prominence given to both processes may well divert the church from concentrating on its primary tasks of mission, evangelism and the nurturing of personal and corporate commitment to its head, Jesus Christ. In other words, we are in danger of fostering distractions from discipleship.

Jesus found it necessary to emphasise to disciples the need for unqualified commitment to him. He asked people to 'take up the cross' and follow him in total obedience. To the man who asked for time to bury his father, Jesus responded sharply: 'Let the dead bury their dead: follow me.' To the disciple who wanted first to say goodbye to his family, Jesus pointed out that 'no man, having put his hand to the plough and looking back, was fit for the kingdom of God'. These were hard sayings, but the message was clear. Distractions from discipleship cannot be tolerated.

Peter was another who found himself on the receiving end of a similar rebuke. Having betrayed jealousy towards 'the disciple whom Jesus loved' and been irritated by Jesus's persistence in questioning his commitment ('Simon Peter, lovest thou me?' he had said three times), Peter asked, 'And what shall this man do?' In effect, Jesus said bluntly, 'mind your own business and don't be distracted by what affects others. *You follow me!*' (John 21:22).

As with the danger of distraction in relation to personal

obedience, so the church must ensure that it is not distracted from its primary aims. 'No sound ought to be heard in the churches, but the healing voice of charity,' wrote Edmund Burke. The church's stated duty is to preach and heal. Its pastoral responsibility is to 'search for the lost, recover the straggler and bandage the hurt' (Ezekiel 34:16, *New English Bible*). The church is built on the rock-like confession of Peter at Caesarea Philippi that 'Jesus is Lord' and so the first duty of the church is to proclaim that message. Of course the church must be concerned about political matters — health, education, justice, poverty, homelessness, war, the proper stewardship of power, the things which affect 'citizens'. If, however, it so concentrates on political involvement that it loses touch with its primary purpose, it has been distracted from its corporate discipleship. The church must use every insight it can gain from psychology and related disciplines, but if that leads to its being no more than a psychotherapeutic clinic, it has been diverted from its fundamental spiritual purpose. The church must engage in social welfare (and there are branches of the church which do it magnificently), but if it ends up being simply a social service it is less than the church ought to be.

Religion, Jesus made clear, is essentially a matter of getting priorities right. If what he calls, in the Sermon on the Mount, the 'other things' (often good things) are promoted to first place and 'seeking the kingdom' is relegated to second place, there have been distractions, whether in personal or corporate discipleship, that disturb proportion. Our inner security and peace depend on getting our spiritual priorities right. That achieved, the 'other things' will fall comfortably into their proper place.

The Divided Self

Internal division is the harbinger of self-destruction, as Jesus made clear to the Pharisees who said his healing work was devilish in origin. How could Satan cast out Satan, he asked. That would be Satan with a divided self. 'Every kingdom divided against itself is brought to desolation,' he pointed out; 'every city or house divided against itself cannot stand'. Former Yugoslavia demonstrates horrendously the truth of that warning as have, down the ages, Ireland, the Holy Land and, in former unhappy days, South Africa. Domestic politics have demonstrated the same truth. Both the Prime Minister and the Leader of the Opposition have taken decisive action at some time because of the risks which internal conflict creates for their parties.

The same danger applies to human beings. Inner conflict can threaten health and well-being. It is not comfortable to be, or to feel like, a divided self.

Such inner tension may manifest itself in various ways. Who has not said at some time: 'Part of me would like to do this, but another part wouldn't'? A fear of loneliness may well compel some people to seek company and social involvement, but deep down the thought of losing their solitude is unbearable. The longing for a permanent, loving relationship may come into conflict with a deep-seated fear of commitment to marriage. Most of the time we can probably cope with conflicts of choice but, at other times, they may lead to worrying indecision or even a paralysing ambivalence.

Inner conflict can come also from the difference between what we *think* and what we *feel*, between our conscious rationality and our irrational unconscious. The pressures coming from the hidden, dark side of our being, feelings unacknowledged or unknown, can force us into behaviour at odds with our conscious intentions. (As St Paul had to confess it: 'The good that I would, I do not, and the evil that I would not, that I do'.) In the realm of sexual misbehaviour, life is littered with personal tragedies that have ended outstanding ministries, brought the public punishment that society demands for unacceptable actions and the removal of talented people from professional registers. Would all who condemn remember that there, but for the grace of God, go any of us!

'Thou desirest truth in the inward parts,' sang the Psalmist. We need reconciliation and healing there too. The divided self, in the sense in which I have used the phrase in this meditation, threatens the fulfilment of that longing for wholeness which is deep in the human soul but, as Bishop Stephen Neill wrote out of his own experience: 'To suppose that Christian life can ever be anything but a conflict is sheer illusion.' Inner tension is to be faced, not feared; accepted, not denied.

The resolution of conflict can be a wholly creative process. For everyone it involves the ancient maxim: 'Know thyself.' For those with faith it involves the glad acceptance of the power promised by Jesus to his disciples, the divine energy, the Holy Spirit.

To become aware of the divided self within us is to move forward on the journey of grace, the end of which is reconciliation, integration, wholeness and therefore inner peace.

The Pilot Light

'And God said, Let there be light, and there was light.' The beautifully told story of the Creation in Genesis records a striking fact. Light was created on the *first* day. Not until the *fourth* day were the two 'great lights' created; 'the greater light (the sun) to rule the day and the lesser light (the moon) to rule the night'. The stars were created then too. Light is therefore the primary element in creation, existing in its own right. No wonder the divine presence is so often described in terms of light! 'God *is* light' John writes and 'in Him is no darkness at all'.

When he wrote the theological introduction to his Gospel, and sought to describe the eternal Word which was 'in the beginning with God', John turned again to the concept of light. John the Baptist insisted that he 'was not that Light' but was sent to bear witness to that Light. 'That was the true Light which lighteth every one that cometh into the world.' It is no surprise then to hear Jesus describing himself as 'the light of the world'.

If light is a form of energy, behaving in certain circumstances 'as if it were a single continuous wave of energy' (my scientific text-book tells me); if all created things are made up of energy, we have a model or image which can perhaps help modern people to conceptualise the notion of spiritual power. *Energeia* is one of the Greek words used to translate the Hebrew word *ruach* (spirit, wind, breath) and is in William Barclay's view more appropriate than *dynamis* (power). Have we not then a highly positive image of the coming of the Holy Spirit, those first disciples filled with the divine 'energy' and transformed into men of conviction, courage and action? With light and energy so related, certain New Testament precepts take on great importance: 'Walk in the light as he [Jesus] is in the light,' says John; 'because Christ shall give you light,' says Paul. Inner light is offered to all as a gift by 'the light of the world'. It is an energising and healing light.

The necessity of the continuing presence of that light within is stressed in Jesus's graphic statement: 'If the light that is in you be darkness, how great is that darkness!' That would mean that our inner light level – our pilot light – had dropped too low for our inner health's sake. The causes may be stress, strain, anxiety, doubt, lack of faith, emotional exhaustion or spiritual dryness. What has happened, writes Agnes Sanford (from whose book *Healing Gifts of the Spirit** I have drawn this image) is that we need, through prayer and waiting on the Holy Spirit, to ensure that our pilot light is re-lit. 'It is from the pilot light all the burners of creativity can be lit, from which our latent abilities and powers are so swiftly brought into new life that we can, indeed, be called a new creation.'

What a blessing is the Old Testament benediction! 'The Lord lift up the light of his countenance upon you.' 'Walk in the light!' for it is the healing light, indeed.

* Published by Arthur James Limited (as is her book, *The Healing Light*).

Lord of the Dance

My abiding memory of Sydney Carter's poem 'Lord of the Dance', set to an old Shaker tune, is of a magnificent rendering of it at the thanksgiving service, in 1993, for the life and work of my wife. Having often shared in the singing of this hymn at conferences, services, weddings and funerals, it came alive as I have never experienced it before, in London's Crown Court Church of Scotland, on that occasion. The poignancy was undoubtedly increased by Sydney's presence with us. Ettie had known him and worked with him over many years.

Sydney is a poet of distinction. His personal search for faith and belief, and the insights he has shared from that probing, have influenced many, not least younger people, and especially the folk-singers of the sixties in whose company he revelled. Who is not aware of his hymn of compassion: 'When I needed a neighbour, were you there?', with its haunting refrain 'and the creed and the colour and the name won't matter – were you there?'. His eightieth birthday was rightly celebrated by an event in Westminster Abbey in May, 1995. He deserves our thanks.

The New Testament has few references to dancing, although Jesus's mention, in the parable of the prodigal son, of the elder brother's anger when he heard music and dancing at the welcome-home party brings no disapproval of it. The Old Testament is much more specific on dancing and very positive. There is a splendid picture of David dancing 'before the Lord', and there are specific exhortations to dance in Psalms 149 and 150 – 'Praise Him in the dance!'

When 'dancing in the aisles' entered (or re-entered) worship in recent decades, many Christians reacted with unease and discomfort. Tradition, temperament and reserve discouraged such phenomena. The charismatic renewal movement, however, with its more spontaneous and less inhibited ways, encouraged arm-raising, 'happy clapping' and expressed affection. In many denominations, too, liturgical dance and movement have more recently been given a place.

It is part of discipleship to love God with 'heart, soul, mind *and* strength', that is with our emotions, spirituality, minds and bodies. The involvement of the physical aspect of us in praise and worship should be seen as positive and creative. Christianity has often been confused and ambivalent over the human body (as problems over sexuality seem to suggest). Yet what more glorious affirmation of the body can there be than that 'the Word was made flesh and dwelt among us'? The Incarnation sets the seal on God's attitude to the body.

'Your body is the temple of the Holy Spirit.' Paul's words determine our attitude to the body and demand that we treat it – ours and others' – with sensitivity. Just this points out the theological difficulty with boxing. If the body is the temple of the Spirit, can it be right, for sport or gain, deliberately to damage the body of another to the point of collapse and even virtual destruction?

'What greater calamity can fall upon a nation, than the loss of worship?' asked Ralph Waldo Emerson in an address to Harvard School of Divinity in 1838. Involving the whole person in worship may well make it a more attractive activity for many.

'Praise Him with the dance' indeed!

See also 'A Time to Dance' (Number 66).

God of Surprises

It is almost impossible to take in the sheer scale of a cata-strophic earthquake, so many thousands killed in such a short time, masses of people injured, the extent of the destruction, the many made homeless. Press photographs, painting in frightening colours the furious fires, present a picture that can only be described as sheer hell. On the scale of human suffering, this natural disaster – added to, it seems, by human failure – must rank high indeed.

There is an article in the Apostles' Creed which proclaims that Jesus 'descended into hell'. It is one that is not easy to understand or interpret. The scriptural references to the descent are in Peter's first letter where Jesus is described as 'preaching to the spirits in prison', and then in Paul's letter to the Ephesians where, in a parenthesis, he comments on a verse from Psalm 68. These do not of themselves explain or clarify the credal statement. We are therefore left to interpret its meaning in terms of our understanding of the whole gospel.

That phrase speaks to me of the completeness of Christ's self-offering on the cross and in the resurrection. The divine love reaches down to and embraces every level of human experience, however awful. It becomes a great and glorious concept, perhaps pointing to Christ's ministering to those who died before his 'redeeming work was done', but certain-ly expressing the comprehensiveness of his saving acts. Paul puts the full impact of that belief into triumphant words: 'Nothing shall be able to separate us from the love of God in Christ Jesus our Lord'. Human beings never find themselves out of the reach of 'love divine, all loves excelling'.

John Greenleaf Whittier expresses that conviction superbly in well-known words:

> I know not what the future hath of marvel or surprise,
> Assured alone that, life or death, His mercy underlies.
> I know not where His islands lift their fronded palms in
>   air;
> I only know I cannot drift beyond His love and care.

If this, the totality of divine love, is real then somewhere in the hell of an earthquake, God is reaching out to people in their dereliction.

Can such a claim be true? Can God really be present in such desolation? It is perhaps one of the divine surprises of faith that it is in 'man's extremity' that God finds greatest opportunity.

'Surely the Lord is in this place and I knew it not.' It was a surprised Jacob who said this in Bethel as he experienced the assurance of God's continuing presence. There, precisely where he was, the ladder, with angels descending to him and ascending to God, spoke to him of the One who keeps faith. 'I will not leave you until I have done all I promised.' There is no hesitation or reservation in that commitment.

Life brings its share of hell to many, possibly at some time to all. It is part of faith to believe in the God who is always there … sometimes to our great surprise.

Part III

In the World

Seven Social Sins

How perceptive, profound and stimulating is Mahatma Gandhi's identification of the 'seven social sins'. Each one is so devastatingly relevant in relation to all we encounter in personal and public life today. If church groups need an agenda for their study of today's weaknesses and problems, let them look closely at these seven sins that affect society now as much as they ever did.

Gandhi's seven social sins are:

> politics without principle,
> wealth without work,
> commerce without morality,
> pleasure without conscience,
> education without character,
> science without humanity,
> and worship without sacrifice.★

The more I read and re-read these words, the more I want to say 'Amen' to them. Not everyone will necessarily acknowledge the truth of each. It would indeed be illuminating to know of possible alternatives. The chosen seven do seem to me, however, to probe deeply into contemporary business, political and ecclesiastical life.

At the heart of religion is a personal commitment, and that is certainly true of the Christian faith. The question put to Simon Peter – 'Who do you say I am?' – produced the great confession of faith which led to Peter being described as

★ Quoted by Jim Wallis in *The Soul of Politics* (Fount Paperbacks, 1995).

'rock'. But emphasis on the need for individual response to the call to discipleship must never hide the corporate responsibilities which are built into being 'the church'. So many words in the vocabulary of faith in the New Testament are 'social' words ... fellowship, community, body, flock and the word church itself. Nor are these cosy words of comfort only. The dynamics of fellowship are expressed in service. The early church had 'all things in common'. The church is not only congregating to worship God. It is called to go from there into all the world in love and compassion.

Added to the responsibilities of the church is the prophetic role, the need to assess and criticise all human institutions, including political ones. The Old Testament prophets set a glorious example of how essential it is to bring the will of God to bear on human programmes and policies, especially when they affect people's welfare.

If the judgement of God on royal behaviour in Old Testament times was one of support and approval, that affirmation was given to kings and rulers. If they disobeyed the divine will, then a resounding 'Thus saith the Lord' would issue forth in a denunciation of self-centredness and self-interest, blatant greed, sexual misbehaviour, sleaze and any policy that was not acceptable to 'the King of Kings and Lord of Lords'. Those who repeatedly refused to 'return to the Lord' encountered the dramatic command: 'Prepare to meet thy God'.

The church today must exercise that prophetic role, encouraging and supporting every policy that makes for goodness and the blessing of people, but bringing the divine perspective to bear on those who commit the social sins.

It would do no harm for all political parties, preparing election manifestos, to consider in depth these social sins as it would be for those who profit from the flawed lives of so-called celebrities looking for pleasure without conscience. As for the church itself, the last of Gandhi's seven social sins should be pondered regularly, namely the irrelevance of worship that does not involve personal and sacrificial commitment.

A Spiritual Blaze

God demands social justice and spiritual integrity. That theme is proclaimed through the Old Testament prophet, Micah, emphasised in the letter of James in the New Testament, and declared, both in Deuteronomy and by Jesus, to be the greatest commandment of all: namely that we must love God with heart, soul, mind and strength, and our neighbour as ourself.

Micah's words on this theme are memorable. God has a case against Israel. Despite the wonder of their deliverance, they were failing in righteousness. But their ultimate salvation depended not on any sacrificial rigmarole designed to placate God, be it thousands of lambs, ten thousand rivers of oil, or even the offering of one's firstborn. God asks not for the gift – but for the givers. Righteousness is expressed in doing justly, loving mercy and walking humbly with God.

James too speaks strongly on social responsibility. True religion, he says, consists of looking after widows and orphans *and* 'keeping oneself from being polluted by the world'; in other words, social service and personal holiness. That is in fact summed up in the Bible's golden rule about the primacy of love.

The demand for social justice and spiritual integrity is relevant today. To do justly, love mercy and respect God are the bases of a healthy society. There are, however, allegations and accusations that threaten the foundations of public life. Political leaders rightly affirm their intention to banish 'sleaze', but public unease will develop into cynicism unless doing justly is seen not as a theory, but as a reality. If confidence in social justice is to be re-established, injustice and deceit must be tackled now. Justice, as Benjamin Disraeli commented, is 'truth in action'.

The obligation to act mercifully is not in conflict with the need for justice. John Milton, like Micah, believes in tempering justice with mercy. This will prevent legalism. Compassion, caring, understanding and support depend on the element of mercy. There are deprived sections of society, the genuinely poor, the shockingly underpaid, the waiting ill, who will only believe in mercy when they experience it, and in compassion only when they feel it.

Social justice and compassion by themselves fall short of constituting 'true religion'. The call to spiritual awareness must also be taken seriously. 'If the world has not approached its end,' writes Alexander Solzhenitsyn, 'it has reached a major watershed in history.... It will demand from us a spiritual blaze; we shall have to rise to a new height of vision, a new kind of life.' We need, indeed, a spiritual blaze!

Governments and oppositions can be pressed to do justly and love mercy, but can they be asked to walk humbly with God? Perhaps not – but individuals can. Democracy will be a different place through the influence of ordinary people demonstrating spiritual blaze.

It is the responsibility of the church to proclaim that message to the world, but it too is bound by the same demand. It must always be seen to do justly, to love mercy and, however difficult it might be, to walk humbly with its God.

Rejoice and Sign!

Rejoice and sign! No, it is not a misprint for 'sing'. Signing is the way in which deaf and deaf-blind people offer their praise to God – as they did at their annual Service of Lessons and Carols* in St Margaret's Church in Westminster, London, before Christmas. To share in such an occasion is moving and encouraging, for the pleasure shown by such people with disabilities in so worshipping God is both manifest and infectious. Because each word has to be made visual, and the words of worship – at least on this occasion – are joyful, there is a radiance demonstrated by hands, eyes and faces not often seen in 'normal' verbal worship.

If those who have a disability can so *en*courage us, why do we do so many things to *dis*courage them? If it is part of religious belief to say that every person is of equal value to God who is 'no respecter of persons'; if we believe that every human being is unique and has the right to develop his or her full potential; if it is a fundamental obligation to have compassion for those whose lives are beset with difficulties, why can we not do more to meet the needs of those with physical limitations? If *we* were to spend just one day in a wheelchair, trying to enter shops, libraries, banks, cinemas, swimming-pools, and coping with domestic duties such as cooking, bathing, cleaning, we might empathise much more with the frustration and desperation engendered in such situations.

Lin, my multi-handicapped friend to whom I have

* Arranged by RAD, the Royal Association in aid of Deaf people, 27 Old Oak Road, London w3.

referred before,† has struggled magnificently with the difficulties created for her by insensitive people and unsympathetic organisations. Writer, lecturer, preacher, therapist, she is also the first multi-handicapped student – cerebralpalsied, blind and in a wheelchair – to complete successfully a basic course in homeopathy. Eight years ago she initiated a trust to deal with something she has often faced – the lack of holiday accommodation equipped to meet the needs of people like herself. £130,000 of the £150,000 needed has already been collected by her, and that holiday cottage, fully equipped, has now been built in East Harling in Norfolk. What a vision! What an achievement!

Much has been done to create public awareness of the needs of people with disability. Toilets, parking, lifts, ramps, doorways and, in some hotels, baths have been provided. Football stadia, following the Taylor Report, have acted positively, as they must, in this matter. The disabled sign is known and recognised. But personal and public blinkers remain, and we create discouragement and distress for those who, though they have disabilities, are due the human rights that belong to all God's creatures.

'Pure religion,' says St James, involves 'visiting the fatherless and the widows in their affliction.' The categories are specific, but his reference to those who are vulnerable implies that compassion and consideration must be shown to all who – for whatever reason – are denied the opportunity to live life to the full.

If that implies money, so be it! It is no credit to a country with a religious background to (in Jesus's word) offend, as it so often does, any of those little – or older – ones who happen to have to cope with a disability.

† I refer to Lin in *Be Still and Know...*, Nos. 21 and 42.

Note: Readers may like to know that over £7,000 was sent to Lin by readers of *The Daily Telegraph* to help her to reach her £150,000 target.

The Lin Berwick Trust is at 9 Hunter Drive, Hornchurch, Essex RM12 5TP

Disability Pride

The debate was due to last for three hours so the capable, caring lady presiding over it helpfully suggested a half-time break 'to give you all the chance to stretch your legs'. But the debate was on disability. On her left, in wheelchairs, were two of the speakers, and several of the audience in wheelchairs too. Everybody, including those with disabilities, laughed because the innocent slip had made a point. How easy it is to use language and images out of habit which, in sensitive areas, can cause hurt.

The question to be debated had been announced as 'Do Disabled People want Christian Healing?' Asked to lead for the affirmative, I refused to assume I could answer this factual question on behalf of people with disability. The right question seemed to me to be: 'Is Christian healing relevant to the needs of people with disability?' Interpreting the healing ministry as I do, the answer had to be an unequivocal 'Yes'. If the purpose of healing ministry is to make people whole in every aspect of their being, the question of disability does not apply. We *all* need healing. On that everyone agreed.

What had given rise to the debate was that some people with disabilities had had it decided for them by individual 'healers' or mass evangelists that they needed to be healed. Some had been exhorted to get out of their wheelchairs and walk. Others had had prayers for deliverance from their disability said over them – without ever being asked if they wanted such healing. What right has anyone to assume that people want to be changed from what they are, and may always have been, into something others describe as 'normal'? There is, after all, such a thing as disability pride!

People with disability may strongly object to that of which they are proud being taken away. 'I am so liberated in my wheelchair!' said an Anglican priest at the debate. 'I am deaf, proudly and profoundly so,' affirmed Dr Mary Weir, a Canadian theologian.* 'Deaf people need each other and need a pride in being who they are as the good creation of a loving God.' It may be a difficult concept but, offered by people with disability, it must be heard.

Our misunderstanding of people with disability may well be due to our attachment to a 'medical model' of disability; that is one which sees people with disability as being in need of 'treatment' so that they can cope better with the world as it is. Ought we not rather to follow a 'social model' which suggests that it is the world and its arrangements that need changing? It is we, society, who disable people by our attitudes.

Jesus dealt sensitively with the rich young ruler who found himself unable to give up his wealth, and refused to force him into discipleship. We alone can decide if we want to change or be changed. It is therefore not for us to try to take away disability, by miracle or otherwise, unless disabled people want us to do so. It is rather our responsibility to en-able those who are different to contribute their unique gifts for the benefit of humanity.

---

* In an address entitled 'Made deaf in God's image' given at an international conference at the University of Kent and quoted in *Disability, Rights and Wrongs* by Ted Harrison (Lion, 1995).

Mites, not Millions

How difficult it is, in an economically ruthless world, to avoid becoming ruthless in order to survive. Greed is an infectious disease and desperately difficult to resist, even by religious people. The national lottery is breeding a new generation of millionaires, funded by ordinary and sometimes poor people, while a £15 million footballer earns £6 every second that he is on the pitch. Yet nurses and similar professions plead in vain for proper financial recognition, patients suffer because funds cannot be found for special treatments, unbelievably low wages are paid in some sectors of society and urgent research into cancer is limited by lack of funds. It really is time to turn away from the 'temporal' purpose of making a million (and the kind of pay-offs and hand-outs that help some to do it) and rather reflect on the 'eternal' importance of the widow's mite.

Let me offer a parable to help recover perspective and priorities, matters on which the New Testament has major things to say. It is a true story that I was told over fifty years ago. How I wish I could remember where this church is!

When the decision was taken to build a new church, everyone in the congregation, including the children, was asked to give sacrificially to help to raise the funds needed. On a certain Sunday the children handed in their gifts, but one little boy looked very unhappy. 'My father is always ill and never works,' he told his teacher, 'so I don't get a Saturday penny, or anything.' Told not to worry, he nevertheless did so, and the following Sunday he handed in a spinning top and five marbles. 'It's all I've got,' he said, 'but you can have it to help build the church.'

When the teacher told the Superintendent about the top and the marbles, he was so moved that he gave ten shillings in the boy's name. The minister was equally moved and increased the ten shillings into a larger gift.

An office-bearer called at the manse that week, was shown into the study, and saw the top and marbles on the desk. Overcome by curiosity, he asked how they came to be there. The minister gladly told him of the sacrificial gift the little boy had made. The office-bearer looked uncomfortable. 'I have already given a large gift to help build the church,' he said, 'but you know I am wealthy and my gift has cost me very little. I will now, anonymously, give another £500 – on one condition: that when the church is built, this top and these marbles will be put on display so that when visitors come to our church they will see them and ask the question I asked you. Then they will be told of the little boy who brought his gift at a cost and, like me, learn the meaning of "sacrificial giving".'

When 'small is beautiful' once more, and sacrificial giving is truly valued, we shall feel that balance has come into the world again. Our perspective might be healthier and our priorities more sound if we concentrated less on millions and more on mites, less on gain and more on giving.

The Primary Task

Jesus, as a Jew, found it natural to refer to, draw on and inter-pret 'the Law and the Prophets'. It is therefore not surprising that he found in the Old Testament a clear definition of his life's purpose.

It happened when he went into the synagogue in Nazareth. Rising to read from the scroll so that he might deliver the portion for the day, he found Isaiah's words star-ing him in the face. He had no doubt of their significance for him: 'The Spirit of the Lord is upon me, because he hath anointed me to preach the gospel to the poor; he hath sent me to heal the broken-hearted, to preach deliverance to the captives, and recovering of sight to the blind, to set at liberty them that are bruised, to preach the acceptable year of the Lord.'

Jesus then sat down and said dramatically: 'That scripture is fulfilled today.'

If the Church is called to be, in a telling phrase (although not everyone feels theologically comfortable with it) an 'extension of the Incarnation', there is no question as to what it has to do. There are three functions that Jesus saw as the prime reasons for his mission. He offered the world a preach-ing ministry, a pastoral ministry (healing the broken-hearted) and a healing ministry (recovery of sight to the blind).

The Church must offer those same gifts to the world. In whatever other areas it is called to witness – politics, social service, public issues, pastoral psychology, industry, econom-ics, ecology (for religion is concerned with the whole of life) – its primary responsibilities are crystal clear, namely to preach and teach a faith: to sustain and develop the spiritual life; to offer pastoral care to all; to exercise a ministry of healing and reconciliation to individuals and to society. The church is weakest when it forgets or sets aside the priorities of its Lord. The Church is at its most dynamic when it applies his principles and reflects his practice.

It is fashionable to dismiss the Church as irrelevant and ineffective, its clergy as answering questions no one is asking. The reality is different. What have I, or any of its ministers, had to do over decades but engage with the facts of life – death and dying, depression and desolation, trauma and tribulation, pain and agony? All of these I have encountered today even as I write these words. To minister to people with understanding and empathy; to meet their deepest needs; to present to them, with sensitivity and strength, abiding truths; what can possibly be more relevant than this?

'Brother, Sister, let me serve you,' wrote hymn-writer Richard Gillman. 'Let me be as Christ to you.' That means being with people where they are. 'I will weep when you are weeping, when you laugh, I'll laugh with you!' Here surely is the truth of the Incarnation. Jesus is 'God with us'.

If the Church properly represents Christ to the world, how can it possibly be irrelevant?

Law and Love

For a definition of anarchy – political, moral or religious – turn to the Old Testament book of Judges where we are told that 'every man did that which was right in his own eyes'. Without a king in Israel, there was no external authority. The result was idolatry and immorality. That definition, where morality and religion are concerned, is not wholly inappropriate today, as recent public and ecclesiastical events demonstrate. The failure of a few does not condemn all but, given the declining influence of religion and a widespread cynicism over politics, external authority is weak. When this happens 'things fall apart; the centre cannot hold,' says W. B. Yeats. 'Mere anarchy is loosed upon the world.... The best lack all conviction, while the worst are full of passionate intensity.'

The historian Arnold Toynbee has noted that disintegrating societies are seldom simply over-run by another civilisation. They tend to commit a kind of cultural suicide. They fall into antinomianism as a substitute for creativeness. People stop believing in morality and yield to their impulses. Tonybee speaks of a consequent promiscuity, not in the sexual sense but in the indiscriminate acceptance of anything and everything, what Gene Edward Veith calls 'an unfocussed eclecticism and uncritical tolerance'.* Toynbee's words touch a nerve today for we are caught in a dilemma. If the church is to be relevant, it is essential that it understand the culture of the times, but to take it too seriously may well

*Quoted and discussed in *Guide to Contemporary Culture*, by Gene Edward Veith (Crossway Books, 1994).

94

lead to a watering-down of the faith and to a syncretism that inhibits effective witness to the Gospel. Where truth is relative, values become relative too. Many will feel that this has already come about, but the alternative often offered is authoritarian fundamentalism of various kinds. Edmund Burke's comment is worth recording: 'Freedom, not servitude, is the cure for anarchy.' It must, however, be freedom with respect for law.

'When the foundations are being destroyed, what can the righteous man do?' asks the Psalmist. It may be that we should look to the relationship between law and love. In both the unhappy case of a bishop with his personal problems, and a political upset years ago, there was manifested a widespread willingness to forgive the human weakness part of the problem. Anger displaced that because of the public lying in both cases. The foundation of 'law', which lays down the rules of behaviour and forbids lying for example, is essential for, without that, society will slide into anarchy. Then there can come into play the law of love with its compassion and forgiveness.

'Remove not the ancient landmarks,' the Good Book says. The time may well have come for society and the church to put traditional markers back into place, markers that have disappeared into the haze created by the proponents not of liberty but of licence. These landmarks established, there is an enormous place in our attitudes and behaviour for the authority of love, the love which (according to Paul) 'never fails'. It is never conditioned by self-interest, real or imagined. It is, of course, the divine love.

Unity in Diversity

Arrogance is the primal sin. That is clearly conveyed by the marvellous Genesis stories of the Creation and the Fall. The divine instruction was clear: 'Do not eat of the tree of knowledge of good and evil.' Encouraged by the 'subtle serpent', they did and the consequences were severe. They included increased pain in childbirth, nature corrupted by thorns and thistles, the toil and sweat now to be involved in creating food supplies, and death becoming a return to dust. And all because our ancestors arrogantly wanted to be as gods.

The story of the Tower of Babel in Genesis 11 makes a similar point. 'Let us build a city with a tower that reaches up to heaven,' said 'the children of men' with inflated egocentricity. The arrogance was too much. 'Let us go down and confuse their language,' said the Lord, 'so that they will not understand each other.' Compulsory diversity and the enforced dispersion of the people is an intriguing punishment for arrogance.

If the babble of many tongues was God's punishment for false pride, there is a different reaction to many languages in another story. The report of events at the first Pentecost, when the promised descent of the Holy Spirit on to the disciples took place, brought a sense of amazement and bewilderment. 'How is it each one of us hears (the disciples) speaking in his own language?' It was a miracle. God was being praised in many tongues. This is surely the unity in diversity of which Paul spoke to the Corinthians. 'The body,' he said, 'is not one part but many.... You are the body of Christ and each one is part of it.'

The principle of unity in diversity is an important one to many fields. It is certainly a lesson that has been learnt in the development of ecumenism. The Church is not best served by a dull uniformity, but benefits most by a true unity expressed in diversity. Every branch of the Church, by its historic witness, underlines some element of truth. We need a corpus of belief shared enthusiastically by all who have one Lord and share one faith, but where contributions from different traditions are received graciously.

The same principle holds good in personal discipleship. Different temperaments need different ways of expressing spirituality. There was no more varied a group than the twelve disciples. Except for one, they were united in loyalty though very different in their attitudes. There is no place in healthy religion for the dogmatism of those who claim that their understanding of the faith is the only right way. People who describe everything that does not agree with their own interpretation as mistaken or, sometimes, even satanic are wholly out of consonance with the image of the free-flowing Spirit expressed in diversities of gifts.

We make our God too small if we suggest that unity is weakened by a proper diversity. Faith, like love, is a many-splendoured thing.

Divine Paradox

It is to the credit of those responsible for the National Health Service that the need for spiritual care is recognised. The Patient's Charter lays it down that 'provider units, including NHS Trusts' should 'make every effort to provide for the needs of patients and staff ... both Christian and non-Christian'. Such public acknowledgement of the spiritual dimension of life is an encouragement to all who believe that coping with suffering and pain demands inner resources. It is therefore a part of modern care to nourish the spirit and so help people cope with the trauma and tragedy that life brings, especially when dreadful things damage and destroy children.

The strongest statement Jesus made was on that very theme: 'Whosoever shall offend one of these little ones that believe in me, it is better for him that a millstone were hanged round his neck and he were cast into the sea.' If only those who load the gun, prime the bomb or contemplate sexual abuse would 'hear' these words, human lives, human hearts, human hopes and human faith would not be shattered by moments of evil madness. The scribbled word 'Why?', lying among the flowers at Dunblane, testifies to that desolation.

Has there ever been such evil in the world as there is today? The answer must be 'No' in terms of quantity (or is it that mass communications brings every human tragedy into our homes?), but 'Yes' in terms of degree. Human beings have always, and often with great cruelty, hurt and harmed other human beings. So far as children are concerned, nothing more monstrous was ever ordained than that royal decree whereby every infant boy under two years old should be slain. The massacre of innocent children by King Herod following the birth of Jesus, is an enormity too awful to contemplate, yet its taking place makes a crucial point for us all in our utter despair over human evil. It was to a world which could perpetrate such an event that Jesus came, to preach, to heal and to love. Moreover, when he who 'went about doing good' was himself the victim (though totally innocent) of an outrageous act of wickedness on Calvary, he left his disciples in no doubt as to their duty. 'Go ye into all the world,' he said, 'and preach the Good News to every creature.' Here is the divine paradox that gives us hope today. It is when the world, in its freedom, can be so evil that there is the need to proclaim the way of love. The deeper the divisions, the greater is the need for reconciliation. The more serious the illness, the greater is the need for healing. When fear and hate pervade the atmosphere it is the more essential to encourage calm and to practise love.

If the National Health Service can recognise the need for spiritual sustenance, how much more should those of a religious faith strive to build up spiritual resources. The ability to survive in the world in which we live and move today depends on personal conviction, inner resources and true serenity. All who believe are under obligation to do all they can to create such strengths in others.

The Call to Care

There is a devastating divine denunciation of the shepherds of Israel in the Old Testament book, Ezekiel. They are, in fact, the rulers of Israel who have failed in their 'pastoral' responsibility to the people. The words of the Lord God are trenchant indeed! 'How I hate the shepherds of Israel who care only for themselves! Should not the shepherd care for the sheep? You consume the milk, wear the wool – but you do not feed the sheep. You have not encouraged the weary, tended the sick, bandaged the hurt, recovered the straggler or searched for the lost.'* This is a serious failure in public stewardship. Might the criticism be relevant to questions relating to our national life today? It is, too, a passage to be taken seriously by the church. If the church and its shepherds, its 'pastors', fail the people in terms of pastoral care, they cannot possibly avoid judgement.

It is a long time ago that I was launched, with no specialist pastoral training at all, into ministerial responsibility for a large congregation containing people experienced in every walk of life. I arrived in my first charge two days before the funeral of an only son, killed in an air accident. That was but the first death in a year of bereavement such as the congregation had never known before. Tragedy followed tragedy. There was, for example, one occasion when I found myself with a senior office-bearer dying in one bedroom, while his wife – unaware of his condition – lay dying in another room. Yet another only son went down with his submarine. A

* Ezekiel 34:2–4 (*New English Bible*).

respected elder collapsed and died on his farm. Such events demanded a level of pastoral skill I could not possibly yet have attained, so I learned pastoral care not in the divinity college, but in the parish. My own faculty of divinity in Edinburgh University is one of those which has led the way in equipping students today to meet the needs of wounded people and the profound problems of society. Whatever help pastoral training can draw from psychology and similar disciplines will enhance its care and should be accepted gratefully.

The church must not, however, turn itself into a psychotherapeutic clinic, any more than it should become a political party or a social service agency because of its concern for political matters such as education, health, homelessness, etc. The church was created to preach the gospel, demonstrate the meaning of fellowship, bear witness to the spiritual dimension so ignored by the world and help its people grow in Christian maturity. Solidly grounded theologically, its function is to be the healing community expressing its love through pastoral care. The 'words of the Lord God,' through Ezekiel (quoted before but well worth recording again), express the wonder of such pastoral care: 'I will go in search of my sheep and rescue them, no matter where they are scattered in dark and cloudy days.... I myself will tend my flock, I myself pen them in their fold. I will search for the lost, recover the straggler, bandage the hurt and strengthen the sick.'* The pastoral task has been delegated to the church. It cannot ignore the call to care.

* Ezekiel 34:12–16 (*New English Bible*).

Sharing in Creation

It is intriguing to read in Genesis that the task of giving the birds and animals their names was allocated to Adam. 'And out of the ground, the Lord God formed every beast of the field, and every fowl of the air, and brought them unto Adam to see what he would call them: and whatsoever Adam called every living creature, that was the name thereof.' The incident is delightful, its significance is profound. *Human beings share in the creativity of God.* What a glorious, hopeful message this conveys! What a vision, not least for the creative arts!

The Creation did not end after seven days, or any specific number of years. God is the Creator still – as miracles, signs and wonders demonstrate. If (as, again, Genesis records) 'God saw everything he had made, and behold it was very good', the same is true of God's on-going creativity. It is our responsibility, as sharers in creation, to do everything we can to ensure that what we create is good too. Then, as St Paul exhorted the Thessalonians, we can 'hold fast that which is good'. That surely is the criterion for assessing the products of the creative arts.

What is, in fact, 'good' requires further definition, for sometimes it is necessary to portray evil in order to demonstrate good. Here, having brought the faith and the arts together, let us consider a quality related to both, that of beauty. 'Worship the Lord in the beauty of holiness' we sing in J. S. B. Monsell's hymn, but there is also the holiness of beauty, with its capacity to move and excite the inner being. To appreciate beauty requires more than that on which, in religious exercises, we so often focus, namely the intellect. We need to involve the imagination, a creative faculty often undervalued today. 'We believe that imagination is stronger than knowledge,' runs a prayer, the source of which I do not know. It continues: 'We believe that myth is more potent than history, that dreams are more powerful than facts. We believe that hope triumphs over experience, that laughter is the only cure for grief. And we believe that love is stronger than death.'

This is not the kind of material on which the tabloid press survives nor is it the diet of politicians, big business and public relations. It will not be regarded as reality in a world in which the trivial is glorified, the irrelevant over-publicised, greed glamorised and possessions celebrated. It is, nevertheless, for those who have the inner eyes to see it, an intimation of reality that takes us beyond the material to the spiritual, that enables us 'to touch and handle things unseen'. It affirms the truth of the Pauline declaration that it is not 'the things that are temporal' that represent ultimate reality, but 'the things which are eternal'.

Let us here rejoice in our call to share in creation and, in so doing, forward the things that are good and lovely.

Creative Illness

Visiting the sick is a responsibility laid on every priest, pastor and minister. It can be a trying and testing experience. I still recall the first case of terminal illness that I met in my first parish. Jane was fourteen and had incurable tuberculosis. I still remember the middle-aged woman in that same period, incredibly deformed by rheumatoid arthritis. Nor can I forget (I am writing of some forty years ago when things were different, medically and socially) the human wrecks gathered together in what was then the 'poor house', cast down, cast out, and cast away by anonymous relations deficient in a sense of responsibility and devoid of humanity. The images remain, as does the sense of failure, with ministry to them all limited because of inexperience of life and an abysmal lack of pastoral training in the divinity college. And yet there was, too, the added blessing that came from contact with people acutely ill and in constant pain. It made such ministry a privilege and an honour.

There is nothing attractive about illness: it is to be avoided where humanly possible. Can one then speak, as Anthony Storr does, of creative illness? He uses the term several times in his book *Feet of Clay* (HarperCollins) when he discusses some famous lives under that title, among them Rudolf Steiner, Carl Jung, Sigmund Freud and Ignatius Loyola. He mentions it particularly in relation to Jung's 'breakdown', an illness from which he learned so much.

It is not easy to sense the benefits of pain when each day of life brings a heavy quota of it (as happens to people I know). One of the benefits of full recovery is the ability to find some blessing in what has been a miserable experience. God does not 'send' suffering, but it is the divine way to so order affairs that good can come out of evil and a blessing out of the burden of illness. Perhaps it has led to a positive change in lifestyle; a transformation of attitude; a corpus of experience that will enable us to minister to others with enhanced compassion and deeper empathy. There are those known to me who, through something as serious as a psychotic episode, have found new life.

Illness brings limitations. It reminds us that we are not omnipotent, but human; that we do not always have the power to control our lives, but can be victims of its strains and stresses. It may lead to a healthy dependence on others and perhaps a greater dependence on divine grace.

Any illness that overtakes us, if we examine it with understanding, may well tell us something about ourselves that can lead to a change in direction, lifestyle and attitudes. None of us wants painful experience, but if and when it comes it may help a little to feel there is the possibility of learning something through it; that there is validity in the phrase 'creative illness'.

Faith, Hope and Love

The image of that Chechen girl, shell-shocked and 'a mask of blood and dust', as *The Daily Telegraph* caption described her, will haunt us for a long time to come. She stands beside the Grozny building battered by an enemy tank. Six adults are dead and many children have been injured. She is desolate. Sadly it is an image that could equally come from Bosnia or Israel as it has done from war-zones of the past – and will in the future. What hopelessness she portrays, incarnating as she does the desolation of war.

Loss of hope is always destructive. That is what makes unemployment a curse and redundancy a disaster. And if the *fact* of redundancy hurts, how devastating is the running *fear* of the loss of one's job. It endangers financial security, family confidence, and quality of life. Young people too, with hard-earned degrees and qualifications, fear for the future. Apparently unvalued by the community, they lack the opportunity to earn, and lose self-respect in the process. So prevalent is this sense of hopelessness that it is eating into the very fabric of society, creating in the collective unconscious emotional dis-ease and anxiety. The public fear of the Chechen girl, and the private worries of ordinary people, are making this indeed a fear-full generation.

Selective text quotation and stock religious language do little to minister to such despair, being perceived as naïve, superficial and unacceptably pious. It is no doubt true, as John says in his first New Testament letter, that 'perfect love casts out fear', but the potential transformation implicit in the text is incredibly difficult to achieve. It is even worse in corporate situations ... family, national and international. What reality does such a statement have, or is it felt to have, where power politics and force of arms are the determining factors? It is the problem all too familiar to 'moral man in an immoral society'. Religious responses can seem academic, doctrinaire, unreal and irrelevant to it.

Yet the responsibility on people of faith to bring light into a dark world persists. If spiritual realities exist as religious people believe they do – and this the more so when Christians proclaim the energy of the Holy Spirit – they have to be brought to bear on human situations. 'More things are wrought by prayer than this world dreams of,' wrote Tennyson. 'After Jesus lived and died,' said J. H. Oldham (in his *Devotional Diary*) 'new and spiritual energy entered into the process of human life.' The great verities remain: *faith*, a personal relationship with God, the power of positive *hope* and the permanency of divine *love*. 'And the greatest of these is love.' 'Love is the sublimest conception available to man' (Oldham again). It is the healing energy for the world.

No text, however profound, can meet the desolation of the Chechen girl or still the anxiety of the frightened unemployed, but all who believe in the spiritual dimension of life must strive to proclaim the wonder of faith, the necessity of hope and the power of love. Within these glorious concepts there is surely some response to despair and desolation.

A New Song

There is a certain irony, unintended as it may be, in football crowds at Wembley on Cup Final day singing a line from the second verse of 'Abide with me'. Henry Francis Lyte seems to equate 'change' and 'decay' when he writes: 'Change and decay in all around I see'. It is not, alas, distant from the truth. Whether it be playing standards, behaviour, public and personal mores, media content, tabloid trivialisation, rampant materialism – there is much that is disappointing 'all around'.

That said, let us immediately banish the view that change means decay. Change is, in fact, a dynamic concept. Responsibly and appropriately approached, it represents a positive, creative, progressive opportunity. It focusses on new attitudes and revised life-styles. Medicine strives to change ill-health into good health. Psychology aims at growth through therapeutic relationship and self-awareness. The aim of politicians is – or ought to be – the creation of a better society. The prime purpose of religion is to offer a way to new life through prayer, relationship, the means of grace, worship, the energy of the Spirit. It seeks to replace doubt with faith, meaninglessness with hope, fear with love. It is therefore not surprising that, in any biblical concordance, there will be a long list of entries under the word 'new'.

Newness of life is a central theme of the New Testament, summed up in the words from Revelation: 'Behold, I make all things new'. There is the *new* commandment Jesus gives the disciples. There is the *new* covenant or testament of which he speaks at the last supper. When anyone comes to be in Christ,

St Paul writes, there is a *new* creation. The exuberant language of Revelation speaks of a *new* Jerusalem and of a *new* heaven and a *new* earth. But the theme is also an Old Testament one in both the Psalms and the prophets. Repeatedly there is the exhortation to sing a *new* song to the Lord. How often the Psalmist affirms with gladness that 'he put a *new* song in my mouth'. When it comes to God's relationship to his people Israel, prophet after prophet registers the promise of a *new* heart and a *new* spirit (Ezekiel), a *new* name (Isaiah), a *new* covenant (Jeremiah). '*New* things I do declare.... Sing a *new* song to the Lord!'

How glorious is the potential of the willingness to change or be changed! How necessary it is in our world today to believe in the possibility of newness of life!

Whether we talk in the language of theology about justification, sanctification, salvation, redemption, grace; or in the language of psychotherapy about growth, maturity, individuation; in human language about joy's triumph over gloom, faith over doubt, hope over anxiety, love over fear, the ultimate theme is the same: 'All thing are made new'. When such enhanced faith is experienced, it will be the easier to join in chorus with the Psalmist:

> You turned my wailing into dancing;
>> you removed my sackcloth and clothed me with joy,
> That my heart may sing to you
>> and not be silent.
> Lord my God, I will give
>> you thanks for ever.*

---

* Psalm 30:11–12, *New International Version*.

Death Hurts

Tennyson's statement that 'death closes all' will, when tragedy comes, find an echo in some people. Others will find comfort in St Paul's assurance that 'death has no more dominion' over Christ and through him, his people. Either way, death hurts. It brings a deep sense of loss whether it comes as relief from long-suffering, as the climax of a fruitful life, as sudden accident or at another's hand in murder or war, or through that most traumatic of experiences, the death of a child. Bereavement brings the need for understanding, sensitivity, support, sometimes closeness, sometimes distance. It is often a time for silence rather than words, presence more than advice, touch rather than texts. There is 'a time to die', but when it comes, death hurts somebody.

I read with sadness a statement made by the National Funerals College which said: 'The average British funeral is a miserable and disappointing affair.' It goes on: 'For those who are not well-known figures or members of churches – most of us – the contemporary funeral lacks meaningful symbolism, dignity, adequate time and comfort for those who mourn.' The College, led by its founder-president Lord Young of Dartington with a United Reformed Church minister, Dr Peter Jupp, as its director, is a body drawn from many areas of society. Its aim is to 'stimulate better funeral practice for the sake of the dead and the bereaved'. It has produced a 'Dead Citizen's Charter', a consultative document for the public and for professionals.

Over the years I have conducted, I suppose, more than a thousand funeral services. Taking any such service is a major responsibility, whether for church members or others, for those who died from natural causes or someone who was murdered, the aged adult or the little child. In time of bereavement, mourners may be overwhelmed by feelings – grief, anger, guilt sometimes, pain always – or find themselves numb and unable to feel anything. Death hurts.

To minister appropriately and effectively to such diverse needs, and in such variable circumstances, involves inner resources. In every funeral, priest, minister or lay person must empathise as deeply as possible with the wounded in spirit; provide comfort and consolation, sometimes forgiveness and reconciliation, always peace and love; convey to everyone the assurance expressed in John Greenleaf Whittier's words: we cannot 'drift *beyond* God's love and care'.

Jesus wept because the death of Lazarus hurt. He can therefore 'bear our griefs and carry our sorrows'. A time limit of fifteen or twenty minutes laid down by crematoria is enough for a service of committal that concludes an act of worship already held in a church, but it can be frustratingly insufficient when that crematorium service provides the only opportunity for generous thanksgiving, pent-up emotion, dignified grieving and unhurried intercession. All who take responsibility for funerals must ensure that, at a time of grevious loss, those who mourn have time both to grieve and to be comforted. People matter when death, whenever and however it comes, hurts.

Lost and Found

The death of a loved one can lead to despair, the death of a child to dereliction, but there are other forms of loss and they too can bring desolation: a breakdown in a loving relationship, the unhappiness of separation or divorce, the loss of a home through repossession, losing personal items in a burglary. Loss and pain inevitably go together.

One of the most moving cries of dereliction in the Bible surely comes from Mary Magdalene, gazing at the empty tomb. It is a heart-broken 'They have taken away my Lord and I know not where they have laid him.' To read that cry of desolation is to feel her grievous pain. It was the loss of the physical presence of one who had meant so much to her that compelled her expression of desperation, but her cry can become the cry of any one of us, as the late Bishop George Appleton put it, dramatically, in a prayer he offered:

> O Christ, my Lord, again and again have I said with Mary Magdalene: 'They have taken away my Lord and I know not where they have laid him.' I have been desolate and alone.

Fortunate are those who have never lost the sense of the transforming union which is at the heart of faith. Many there are, however, who have known that loss and been made desolate by it.

J. B. Phillips, describing the 'darknesses and depressions' he knew so well in later life, felt that a key factor in their affecting him was the acceptance of 'hundreds of demands made on my time which were out of all proportion to my real strength'. Others may link their lost spirituality to their inability to overcome the 'false self' formed in early years, and later to be the source of, in religious terms, temptations. Some too may feel that the rampant materialism and secularism so typical of life today is responsible for the development of a spiritual aridity that makes the pursuit of (as Jesus called them) the 'other things' a priority rather than 'seeking first the kingdom'.

In our church life we may, like Martha, be 'careful and troubled about many things' – meetings, organisations, activities – and obliterate attention to that 'better part' to which Mary attended and which Jesus commended. Over-concentration on the correctness of liturgy or the intricacies of theology, both valuable disciplines, can obscure for some the essential simplicity of the gospel and hide the Jesus who is present in true worship. The genuine desire for contemporary ways of 'conceptualising' God and the search for appropriate images in place of traditional but irrelevant ones can, as a by-product, create confusion for those with a simple faith. 'Where is Jesus now?' they cry.

There is no need, however, for loss of hope. 'I am desolate and alone,' prayed Bishop Appleton, who then added triumphantly: 'But you have found me again!' It is not on our grasp of God that the transforming union depends, but on God's grasp of us. The prodigal son found in a waiting, welcoming father the assurance that the relationship he thought he had lost was still there, strengthened through his desolation.

Life after Death

'For what is it to die but to stand naked in the wind and to melt into the sun? And what is it to cease breathing but to free the breath from its restless tides, that it may rise and expand and seek God unencumbered?' So wrote Khalil Gibran in *The Prophet* (Heinemann). The words are moving and the concept glorious. The poet-philosopher from the East proclaims the transforming power of death: 'Only when you drink from the river of silence shall you indeed sing.' The same promise comes from the New Testament. Death has 'no more dominion' over humankind. It is, declared Paul, 'swallowed up in victory'.

This is a faith which has sustained many on their journey through life, but is it an affirmation of the ideal or a denial of the real? Death is of today. When it comes as quickly, cruelly and violently as it may, it brings the agony of bereavement and the deep pain of loss. Be it in the humble home where the beloved partner is suddenly taken; in a plane crash, rail disaster or avalanche; in a hospital ward or as the result of indefensible cruelty in a prison camp; in the obscenity of the holocaust; in the bombing by an aircraft or in the searing blast of an atomic bomb destroying thousands – this is the reality of death. It is not easy to see the great vision through trauma, tears and torment. Can death be healing?

Death, it is often said, is today's taboo topic. Is it that it is too difficult to face, and so is set aside, denied, repressed? It was not in the divinity hall but in the parish that I encountered the pastoral needs of the bereaved. I was taught Hebrew, Greek, divinity, dogmatics, ecclesiastical history –

but nothing dealing with dying and death. It is better now. There are many training courses for all on loss and bereavement. And there are individual teachers too, such as Elisabeth Kubler-Ross who 'brought death out of the closet' in her seminars on Life, Death and Transition. Sadly, following a series of strange events which included the destruction of her home, office, books, papers, equipment, etc., and then a stroke, such workshops are over. Other bereavement organisations remain and develop – for example, Cruse, the Compassionate Friends (a self-help organisation for those bereaved of their son or daughter through any cause), the marvellous hospice movement. To bring together the reality of death with a theology of hope remains a priority task in our times.

Blessed indeed are those who minister to the dying and the bereaved, who sit where those in grief and pain sit, who offer not theory but practical compassion, empathy and love, who bring to those enveloped in the darkness of desolation, a glimmer of light. Death is not an end but a beginning. 'When you have reached the mountain top,' says Gibran, 'then you shall begin to climb. And when the earth shall claim your limbs, then shall you truly dance.'

Power to Change

Jesus understood the feeling of helplessness. However strange it may seem to say this of one to be called 'Son of God', the Gospel records make clear his sense of impotence in certain situations. 'O Jerusalem, Jerusalem,' he cried to the city over which Luke tells us he shed tears, 'how often would I have gathered your children together and you would not!' Human intransigence had made him helpless, as it had done in 'his own country'. 'He did not many mighty works there because of their unbelief.'

It is such a relief to know that Jesus wept, for it proclaimed the reality of his humanity and showed him to be 'God with us'. To find Jesus experiencing feelings of helplessness underlines that humanity and his ability to identify with people. If there were things that he could not change, how much more are *we* in that situation!

It is the unbearable sight of human suffering in so many places, where people seem to have descended into hell, that moves me to reflect on helplessness. How utterly impotent we can feel in the face of such pain! Thanks be to God for those who risk life and limb, health and future, to minister to the sick and dying. For most of us, the sense of limitation can be overwhelming. We can pray, of course. We can give gifts. Beyond that, it is no more than a deep yearning ... if *only* we could really help. But we are not omnipotent. There are things we cannot do. Even our capacity to take so much suffering into our hearts is limited. Helpless ourselves, we cannot help the helpless.

To admit our limitations is not weakness, it is realism. It

reminds us that there are unchangeable situations in life for which the only solace is in the doctrine of forgiveness. We must not feel guilty because we cannot ameliorate all the world's suffering. There *is* emotional pain for which we cannot find balm, illness we cannot cure and death in relation to which we can arrange no resurrection. Yes, there are things we cannot do.

Such realism is however no excuse for despair. What is important in the life of Jesus is not the few things he could not do, but the record of what he did. His impact is in the signs and wonders he effected; in the changes in people which he wrought; in the new lives he created. It was the politics of Robert Louis Stevenson 'to change what we can, to better what we can'. It must also be our religion.

It is realistic and right to recognise our limitations. It is, however, much more important to be sensitive to the promised power of the Holy Spirit, that energy of God which turned weak and frightened disciples into world-changers. There is so much that can be different and better through the grace that is sufficient for all our weakness. It was people perceived as helpless who were given the power to be positive and productive in proclaiming the possibility of new life. Be encouraged by that!

Faith and the Arts

That fine Scottish actress and comedienne Molly Urquhart once told me how hurt she felt when, determined to go on stage, she was ostracised by her rigid, Calvinistic parents for choosing such a career. Going into the theatre was, for them, 'going to the devil'. It is sad that she should be a victim of the sort of relationship between the church and the arts that so often in the past created such bitter barriers. For that conflict, both sides must share the blame.

Many people in the churches have felt strongly that drama in the theatre, cinema or on television has deeply undermined public standards and family life. In particular they have felt uneasy over (formerly) implicit and (more recently) explicit sexual behaviour, normal and abnormal, over the aggressive use of unacceptable language, and, especially within late-night television, a seeming fascination with deviation and perversion. At the same time producers, directors, actors and actresses seem to claim for their profession a mystique that compels them to claim total freedom in artistic matters and, in doing this, damage the sacredness of intimate relationships and besmirch holy things.

'Art deals with life, death, love, sex, everything that makes the world go round' Sandy Nairne of the Tate Gallery is quoted as saying. It is perhaps in relation to the exploration of frailty, despair and degradation that church and arts may disagree. The arts seek *carte blanche* in presenting life as it is, in all its horror and obscenity, individual and corporate, public and private. The church may consider there is too great an element of risk in such portrayal, but it must also try to understand the integrity, where it is genuinely present, of artists, writers and directors in their believed pursuit of that which is good. After all, the church of the Bible is familiar with the need for risk in exploration. 'Launching out into the deep' at Jesus's command produced a miracle. The children of Israel reached the promised land because their ancestor, Abraham, in obedience to God 'went out not knowing whither he went'.

The conflict between the arts and the church is unnecessary and destructive. Both are primarily concerned with the creative, the good and the beautiful. 'Beauty,' said Dostoyevsky, 'will save the world.' It is too great a claim, as Alexander Solzhenitsyn agrees, but he adds: 'There is a special quality in the essence of beauty.... The old trinity of Truth, Good and Beauty is not just the outworn formula it used to seem to us....' There is so much common ground. 'Art and faith are concerned with what it takes to be human and with transcending the boundaries of human life,' writes Donald Smith, Director of the Church of Scotland's Netherbow Theatre and the John Knox House Museum in Edinburgh. 'Art satiates the need for human values' (Sandy Nairne again) 'in an age when everything is transitory.'

The case for co-operation rather than competition between faith and the arts is strong. They should not be, as Molly Urqhuart found them, bitter rivals, but rather colleagues in the creation of that which is 'good and lovely, and of good report'.

Urgent Persuasion

There is a verse in Luke's Gospel that appears to authorise force to bring about religious commitment. St Augustine was one, and there were many others, who used it in this way. The reference is, of course, to the words spoken by a 'certain man' in Jesus's parable about the great feast: 'Compel them to come in.'

The host, having received many apologies for declining his invitations to supper, asked his servant to ensure that every place at his table was occupied. A foray into the city streets and lanes was only partially successful although it produced a number of guests, some physically handicapped. The host, furious, sent his servant to search the highways and hedges outside the city to provide yet more guests. It was then that the crucial words were spoken: 'Compel them to come in,' he said (Luke 14:23).

I checked fifteen commentaries on the use of the word 'compel'. All were unanimous that it did not imply physical force. The translators confirmed this. Synonyms like 'urge', 'make', 'strongly encourage', etc., were employed. The concept is much more that of (as one commentator summed it up) 'urgent persuasion'.

There are highly relevant contemporary issues relating to evangelistic methodology in those words. Response to the gospel is, of course, a matter of urgency. But are there boundaries which one has no right to cross in 'evangelising' another person? Are there limits to what is acceptable in urgent persuasion?

Diversity is of the Spirit, Paul told the Corinthians. Every permissible form of communication must be used to meet the varied needs, temperaments, age-groupings and cultures of today. The gospel must be proclaimed and spirituality must be expressed in ways appropriate to contemporary youth culture. The challenge is to find the limits to what is acceptable.

Jesus, in his encounter with the rich young ruler, offers us a model for evangelistic endeavour, implicitly indicating the limits in persuasion permissible. He presented unequivocally to the rich young ruler the implications of a commitment to discipleship, but made no effort to force him to a decision. He loved him – and let him go.

The church must not be seduced by the need to attract thousands as some religious enterprises do. Recognising that small can be beautiful, that the glory of the Old Testament was not mass obedience but the reliability and faithfulness of the remnant, that Jesus set out to build the Kingdom of God with but twelve disciples (including one seriously flawed and others who were weak), it must adhere to its responsibility to present to the world a way of life grounded in Jesus Christ, to 'preach the gospel', that is, make known the offer of that gospel and leave the response to those challenged by it. What is also clear is that a caring, loving life, so grounded, may still be the most effective influence of all.

The Risks of Giving

Jesus left his followers with severe problems! Take, for example, the obligation to respond to human need. John deals in depth with this theme – compassion as the consequence of salvation – in his first epistle. 'If a man has enough to live on and yet when he sees his brother [or sister] in need shuts up his heart against them, how can it be said that the divine love dwells in him?' (1 John 3:17, *New English Bible*). The logic of that cannot be gainsaid. 'If God so loved us, we ought also to love one another.'

Jesus's exhortations on compassionate response to another's needs are in the Sermon on the Mount. They are concise and specific. 'Give to him [or her] that asketh thee and from him [or her] that would borrow of thee, turn thou not away.' That statement, moreover, is made in proximity to his exposition of the principle of the 'second mile'. Compassion is expressed in a doubled generosity in response to pleas. But how do we apply these instructions, given in a simpler world, in our modern, complicated situations?

When I visited St Stephen's Cathedral in Vienna, I read among the rules applying to attitude, attire and behaviour 'in this place of worship', a specific further injunction. It ran: 'Do not give alms to professional beggars.' That is indeed the rub – as was confirmed a few days earlier in a hotel in Budapest when an Irish teacher commented on this very problem. 'I saw a man in Dublin with a poster round his neck,' she said. 'It proclaimed: 'I am hungry and homeless.' But I *knew* the bloke! He lives near me, in a normal house!'

That sense of helplessness of which I have written in other

connections* can be very real over response to need. Yet moved to compassion we still must be – by the old Hungarian peasant, crouched on the pavement, outside the church in Pest; by the eleven-year old boy on crutches, waving his begging-tin before all the passengers on the Metro in Buda; by (although we have been officially warned) the young woman with the baby on the London Underground. Yet how difficult it is to turn away from such misery. And, in the corporate field, the appeals, three a day on average, roll in – Rwanda, Bosnia, multiple sclerosis, cancer, and so on. All are overwhelmingly urgent needs, but our capacity for practical compassion is so severely limited.

There is, at the heart of our faith, a belief in the infinite value of every human being, made in the image of God. That some turn out to be frauds is no reason to close down the innate compassion of the loving heart. The risks of giving are an integral part of the risks of loving – and there are many. It may be that, in the naïveté and innocence of our reactions, we become 'fools for Christ's sake', but we dare not 'shut up our hearts' against those in need.

There is a parable – about sheep and goats – which spells out the dangers of ignoring the needs of 'one of the least of these', our brothers and sisters of Christ.

* See Number 48, 'The Power to Change'.

Common Ground

'Be still and know that I am God' is a text which says much about the relationship of silence to the sense of the presence of God. I therefore find it difficult to think of noise as the medium of the divine message.

I felt that problem acutely when I attended a Mission to London meeting in the Earls Court arena. Thousands came each night to hear Morris Cerullo's preaching. It was a proclamation of the gospel that declared the faith, sought conversions, demanded commitment and encouraged the Christian life. The core message was the wonder of God's love, the transformation brought about by encountering Jesus and the power of the Holy Spirit. To all that, I offer an enthusiastic 'Amen'. It is not, however, the message which creates difficulties. It is the method.

The mission offered traditional evangelistic endeavour accompanied by the usual components of mass evangelism – music, choir, soloist, confrontational preaching, 'going forward', the appeal for money, etc. What was new to me was the setting of the exercise in a pop concert genre. That meant three hours (one of 'build-up', two of meeting) of unremitting noise – voices, music, the solo trumpet used (skilfully) by the associate evangelist (who preached the night I was there) to emphasise his message, all efficiently amplified. There was, too, the response of the thousands present, a singing, swaying addition to the total volume of sound.

It was patently clear that the whole experience brought to many of the young people around me, inspiration, affirmation and genuine spiritual joy. God, it seemed, was present in the incessant noise and flashing lights. Yet somehow, deep down, I felt the lesson Elijah learned was an important one. He did not, as he expected, find God's presence in the drama of earthquake, wind and fire. It was in the silence that he had to listen to the still, small voice.

There has always been a gulf between older and younger generations, but that gulf has never been greater than it is now. Technologically confused grandparents seem to inhabit a different world from their computer-literate grandchildren who move serenely through the maze of information technology and enter easily (though not without the danger of addiction) into the world of Internet. While traditional religious language meets the needs of many (but not all) older people, young people need to express their spirituality through their own culture and vocabulary. There is however, in terms of faith, common ground. Jesus is the same 'yesterday, today and for ever'. For older and younger, the crucial question is the same. It is the one put to Peter by Jesus: 'What do you make of Christ?'

The response can only be offered individually and will be expressed in concepts and language belonging to the generation to which each belongs and within the milieu in which they are at ease. For some that will be the silence of the desert place, for others it will be amid the noise of so-called 'rave culture' services.

It is, I believe, in the quiet moment that the wonder of the divine love is revealed. Following the miracle of grace there is, of course, every reason to shout 'Hallelujah!'

The Torpor of Indifference

Repetition, when properly used, can be very effective. In the book of the Old Testament prophet Amos, there is a good example of repetition used for emphasis. Five times the God of Israel says: 'Yet have you not returned unto me.' 'Yet' is the crucial word. Though judgements have been 'sent' by God, one after another – famine, drought, destruction, pestilence, defeat – Israel just will not respond and repent. Words of inevitable doom follow: 'Prepare to meet thy God, O Israel.'

I once asked a colleague to read this passage from Amos at morning worship. She flatly refused, on the grounds that any God 'sending' such punishments was not the God she knew in Jesus. I respected her feelings and changed the reading, but the responses to the judgements recorded in this passage point to something important to the spiritual life. It is the phenomenon of the hardening heart.

'A wicked man hardeneth his face,' says the writer of the Proverbs. The hardening face (male, female or group) is the exterior expression of the hardening heart, so graphically illustrated in the case of Pharaoh, king of Egypt. After each new plague sent in judgement, he 'hardened his heart' and still refused, as Moses said, to 'let my people go'.

If the language sounds old-fashioned, the phenomenon itself is wholly contemporary. There is today an over-acceptance of, and indifference to, wrong-doing. It is another form of the hardening heart expressed in insensitivity to evil. The violence, featured so much in the media, is seen as a 'normal' part of society, a fact we acknowledge as we avoid the fear-full streets and create our fortress homes. Language once banned from radio and television is now a regular part of, especially, late-night programmes. 'When I was a young man,' said the late Professor Jack Perry, the authority on trading with China, responding to eightieth birthday tributes, 'I did not know anyone who was divorced.' Recalling his seven-year 'courtship' of his wife, Kate, he contrasted such a practice with the instant relationships of today and the reduced stability they bring. In so many fields, standards have deteriorated, values have been undermined and the gentle graces discouraged. What we would have denounced yesterday is acceptable today. That is the subtle deterioration evident in our society. It is this insensitivity to grace and goodness which, in this widespread unawareness of them, is the contemporary expression of the hardened heart. We are indifferent to that process at our peril.

Indifference is a dangerous and an infectious disease. Untreated, it develops into something worse. 'There is nothing so fatal to religion as indifference,' wrote Edmund Burke in 1795. 'It is, at least, half infidelity.' It is not open hostility the faith has to fight today. It is (in the words of John of Salisbury) 'the torpor of indifference'. It is that which leads to the hardening of the spiritual arteries today.

'I know thy works that they are neither cold nor hot,' was the judgement made on the church of the Laodiceans (in the book of Revelation). 'Thou art merely lukewarm.' Apathy, indifference, insensitivity, the hardened heart – these are the current symptoms of estrangement and alienation from spiritual resources. It is time to 'make all things new'.

The Way to Renewal

The Church dare not try to demonstrate its need to be 'relevant' by reducing its standards, lowering its personal demands or accommodating its beliefs to contemporary criticisms. In other words, it will not fulfil its purposes by, in Paul's words to the Romans, being 'conformed to this world'. Its function is exactly the opposite. It is to 'transform' the world.

The *presentation* of the Church's beliefs is a different matter. Of course it must avail itself of technological advance and modern methods of communication, accepting that many people (and most children) are used to visual aids in their education. Where the medium of the message is concerned, the Church must be contemporary indeed. But the message itself – that remains constant. Jesus Christ *is* 'the same yesterday, today and for ever'. All that is needed for salvation and wholeness is in the gospel. Christianity is best served when it presents itself as it is, stressing its call to commitment and personal sacrifice. Significantly, those churches which underline the demands of discipleship are the growing churches. Those that do not tend to wither away.

I had the privilege of leading a weekend retreat for a village parish church. It was a 'family weekend' held at a conference centre some distance from the congregation's home base. For various reasons, that church had had lean years and its work and witness had decreased. Morale in the congregation was low. Then arrived their dedicated and gifted young minister and his wife and a remarkable renewal has taken place, quantitatively and qualitatively. The gathering was made up of young couples, families, young people, older people. All were enthusiastic about the church and its purpose and unanimous about the minister's part in the church's growth and the deepening of its spiritual life.

After the event, I found myself reflecting on the underlying reasons for this impressive development and identified three crucial elements in it. They were the emphases placed on *preaching, prayer* and *pastoral concern.* Yet there was no off-putting over-earnestness involved and no false piety. There was real fellowship and plenty of fun. The core of the renewal process did however clearly lie in a sound preaching and teaching ministry, a commitment to personal and corporate prayer and real *koinonia,* that is, fellowship expressed in mutual pastoral concern.

The Church must be the church. It must do the things to which it is primarily called. The gospel must be proclaimed. Prayer must be offered. The love of God must be made incarnate in pastoral care. There is in that congregation much activity of other kinds – social concern, shared leisure activities, local outreach, etc. – but the three identified factors are now and will always be their priorities.

There are, of course, many churches across the country equally relevant and showing similar growth. I focus on this one example because I was there to see what can happen where it is accepted that there is the word to be preached, a corporate spiritual life to be developed and a fellowship of love to be actively demonstrated; where, in fact, the church is the Church.

Things New and Old

'Ordination is not a licence to do violence to a congregation.' That statement, made in 1980 by the Church of Scotland's Panel on Worship in a publication called *New Ways of Worship*, merits careful reflection by anyone called to ministry. The responsibilities of ordination are not to be taken lightly.

When I was at boarding school we were sent each Sunday morning to a local church. I recall clearly the sweat on the brow of that minister and his nervous fiddling with the corners of the pages of his pulpit Bible as he strove to cope with the demands of his office. The responsibility of leading a group of people in worship (be it a thousand, or 'two or three' gathered together) and proclaiming the will of God to them is, as it was for the prophets of old, nerve-racking.

Preaching is a function which is not for the private advantage of the preacher, but for the blessing of the hearers. The pulpit must not be used to expound personal prejudices or political views, nor should its hidden purpose be to meet one's own inner needs or satisfy individual interests. The proclamation must, of course, be channelled through the personality of the preacher. So long as the content is safeguarded by reference to 'the supreme rule of faith and life', the Bible, freedom in the Spirit is real. The living word can never be imprisoned within inflexible dogma or formal creeds. The Spirit, Jesus tells us, blows where it chooses. So long as the preacher is consciously dependent on that Spirit, given to prayer and concerned to build up the faith of the people, he or she has freedom. The preacher's calling is onerous indeed, but it is privileged. It is, after all, about the cure of souls.

The same degree of responsibility exists in relation to the conduct of worship. The desire to be freed from rigid, fixed orders of service, so as to make worship relevant, is a proper aim. It should not , however, become as it sometimes does, directed to amusement and entertainment rather than glorifying God and blessing people. The words of the Panel of Worship of the Church of Scotland are wise indeed: 'The recurring task of those who conduct worship may be seen as similar to that of the householder in the parable (Matthew 13:52) who was expected to "produce from his store things new and old". In worship, it is the old which provides continuity with the past and allows one generation to speak to another. But to turn to another parable (Matthew 11:17), we must also pipe to this generation in airs it recognises and with music to which it has grown accustomed, if people today are to join in the dance of the divine service.' How true!

Those called to ministry have a responsibility from which they cannot abdicate. The reactions of 'my' early minister were perhaps exaggerated, but completely understandable – and right. It is demanding to be called to be the bearer of the good tidings of the gospel.

Part IV

Times and Seasons

Pardon, Power and Peace

The question is not whether the Church is relevant today but whether most people feel it to be relevant to them. My instinctive reaction to that latter question is a 'No', a reaction somewhat confirmed by the presence of but six of us at the early morning Eucharist in a parish church on Christmas Day. But other factors bring that judgement into question.

For example, a pre-Christmas survey found that 41 per cent of those interviewed said they might well go to church during the Christmas period. Carol services obviously inflate this figure but, compared with accepted average levels of church attendance in this country, that is a remarkable percentage. It surely says something about the felt need for contact with the Christian faith today. An earlier survey, moreover, showed that in 1994 the percentage of those who were more concerned with the spiritual aspects of Christmas than with the commercial and social aspects had increased significantly since 1993.

These insights suggest that, although the institution 'church' – with its own language, thought-forms, traditions, 'ecclesiasticism', concern with theological minutiae, etc. – may not seem relevant to many people (though many Christians, clergy and lay, work hard, sincerely and with imagination to make it so), the desire for faith and grace draws people towards that for which the Church stands, the gospel of Jesus Christ. There is a sense that, within religion, personal needs can still be met, and perhaps increasingly so. There is a relevant faith for today available to all and, deep down, many people know it. The word 'relevant' comes from a Latin verb meaning 'to raise up', 'to relieve'. It is (the dictionary says) 'associated with the notion of helping'. To be relevant, then, means having the capacity to bring relief to people, to raise spirits, to encourage. The Christian faith is relevant today because it can respond to real and deep human needs ... the longing for a new beginning, that second chance, perhaps even Jesus's 'seventy times seven' level of forgiveness. The experience of that forgiveness and the new opportunity it brings is the most healing aspect of a faith founded on the belief that God is Love.

Inner peace will not solve the problems of the world or even our personal problems but, with the gift of that peace which, Jesus said, 'the world cannot give or take away', it is more possible to cope with them. And for those who need resources, the promised, transforming spiritual power experienced by the disciples at that first Pentecost remains on offer to all who ask for it.

There is a faith for today that offers pardon, peace and power to all who seek it. The church must do all it can to ensure access to it for all who want such blessings.

What Perversity!

'The modern generation has no faith. There is a fatal perversity about it.' Those words bring unhappy images into my mind. I see those huge advertisements designed to encourage (as it seems to be believed) a gullible public to smoke more, advertisements which at the same time carry (but only because by law they must) the chilling reminder that smoking causes cancer, and cancer brings death. What perversity is this! I read of terrible atrocities in Africa, and learn from a *Sunday Times* report that a British company has exported machetes to one of the sides involved in the butchery. Of so much arms trade it seems appropriate to say, 'What perversity is this!' John Rae's words in *The Custard Boys* touch a painful nerve: 'War is, after all, the universal perversion. We are all tainted; if we cannot experience our perversion at first hand, we spend our time reading war stories, the pornography of war; of seeing war films, the blue films of war....' We condemn violence, rightly seek to ban guns and knives, yet in any evening's television, violence with knives or guns will almost certainly be featured. 'You live in an age which is twisted and perverted' I read, and in our despairing moments, we fear we do.

The words with which I began, however, are not a statement about today – although they could be. *They are the words of Jesus to the people of his generation.* Paul writes to the Philippians as people living in an age 'in which life is twisted and perverted'. It simply leads to one conclusion. Human nature does not change. It is perverse indeed.

What does 'perversity' mean? Contradiction, stubbornness, being wrongly self-willed, directed away from what is right or good, my dictionary tells me. It is the kind of condition of which St Paul talks in the passage to which I refer so often: 'There is a law in our members that when I would do good, evil is present with me.' And why does this theme – perversity – affect me so much now? Because it is so demonstrated in Jesus's journey towards Calvary.

Take Palm Sunday, for example. What perversity is this that Holy Week begins with the triumphal entry into Jerusalem and ends with Jerusalem crying 'Crucify him, crucify him!'

Take the choice of Barabbas as the one to be freed, Jesus the one to be condemned. They liberate a murderer. They murder a holy man. What perversity is this!

See Pontius Pilate proclaiming Jesus's innocence, washing his hands and – despite his wife's warning – delivering Jesus to be crucified. What perversity is this!

Such perversity is caused by the fault that runs through human nature. It is the product of human disobedience and wilfulness. And to the human dilemma there is but one answer. It is the transformation of perversity, through divine forgiveness and grace, into positive faith and commitment.

To help achieve that blessing has been the purpose of the Lenten pilgrimage with Jesus.

The Lenten Privilege

Lent is a time of opportunity. Observing it in the appropriate devotional spirit enables us to focus on the great events of Jesus's life and their relevance for our lives. The Lenten pilgrimage provides the stimulus for a determined and disciplined effort to concentrate on spiritual growth. We should grasp that opportunity.

Progress in the spiritual life is a gift of grace, but the grace comes only if we create the prepared context in which to receive it. To hear what God will say means deliberately being in a position to listen. To do what God requires us to do is dependent on our expectant attention. Jesus discouraged 'much speaking' in prayer. He encouraged the simplicity of genuine faith. The quality of the devotional life is not determined by the number of hours or minutes we spend in prayer and meditation, but by the capacity to receive and obey, to watch and wait, to assimilate and act. The child Samuel articulates the proper response for all of us: 'Speak, Lord, for thy servant heareth.'

Waiting on God demands dedication, discipline and concentration. But, as Hamlet would say in another context: 'Ay, there's the rub.' How hard it is to concentrate in the stillness, for any length of time, on spiritual things! There are always those dreaded distractions – tomorrow's problems, family demands, mounting bills, undefined anxieties – the fears and worries that are different in degree and detail but are common to us all. It is inevitable that the pressures which dominate life in a stressful world, and which occupy much of our waking attention, should break through into that time

138

reserved for deeper contemplation. It is a human problem, not a sin.

Those who practise meditation find that there are helpful ways of trying to defeat distraction. Some, for example, take an object – a flower, a candle, a familiar symbol, an appropriate picture – so that whenever the mind begins to wander it can be quickly brought back to the focus of spiritual attention. Some take a passage from the Bible and are ready to return to it if external thoughts intrude. Some hold a verse or a text in mind – 'Be still, and know that I am God,' or 'Jesus is Lord,' for example – repeating it in mantra form to aid concentration.

It was of Principal D. S. Cairns' spirituality that his son, Professor David Cairns, wrote movingly and inspirationally: 'My father has left the outsides and circumferences of those who write about the meaning of things, and he is bent at the centre, to see with his own eyes and touch with his own hand the pearl of great price.' He was indeed focussed fully on the Kingdom, and unlikely to be distracted by unimportant things.

We travel far behind the saintly Cairns on the spiritual journey, but at least we can sense the aim of it. Whatever distracts us in our quiet times needs setting aside, and that not with over-earnestness but with good humour. The Lenten privilege of doing all we can to 'keep looking unto Jesus' is time well spent.

A New Beginning

Lent originally meant spring. The festival that runs from Ash Wednesday to Easter really, then, relates to new life and spiritual growth. The popular association of Lent with 'giving up' something, while rightly pointing to the need for Lenten discipline, becomes too narrow a concept, for the real Lent is a time of sanctification and inner growth through self-examination, contrition, forgiveness, renewal, commitment and the restoration of 'the soul's sincere desire'. Journeying with Christ towards his death and resurrection and feeling the purpose and pain of that journey ministers to the spirit and nourishes wholeness. It is a time to take seriously Paul's exhortation to the Philippians to 'fill your minds with ... the things that are good and lovely and of good report', that is, worthy of praise; in other words with the beauty of holiness.

Striving for personal holiness in the world of today is an enormous task. Evil seems to be so prevalent and pervasive – and so infectious. 'Sleaze' in politics and 'bungs' in sport are part of a new and unpleasant vocabulary. The level of what is acceptable in entertainment slips ever downwards and, recently, dramatically so. There are series which trawl the gutters of human behaviour in the name of novelty and comedians whose only stock-in-trade seems to be dirt. This is not a call for censorship. It is a plea for self-discipline, for licence is liberty without discipline. It is the licence that says 'anything goes' which is sought today. We are allowing a downward spiral to evolve and take us to levels from which it will be difficult ever to return.

The cultivation of the beauty of holiness is a genuine

Lenten task, both individually and corporately. There is a responsibility laid on all, whatever their religious stance, to proclaim in their words and to present in their life-style the beauty of holiness, a holiness not prudish and restrictive but healthy and wholesome, a holiness which values the good and the lovely, the things worthy of praise.

It must be a matter for concern that so much that is trivial, trashy and tawdry is shaping the ambience in which young lives evolve today. Only in contact with the truly holy – that is the good and the lovely – can spiritual growth develop into maturity.

Nowhere is the value of influence more demonstrated than in the doctrine and practice of infant baptism. To take vows, consciously and deliberately, to ensure that a child is brought – through membership of Christ's body, the church – within the sphere of holy happenings and holy things is to bless that child's future. However unaware consciously of the grace that is mediated through the sacrament, that child is in contact, if vows are fulfilled, with the wonder of goodness and the people of faith who try to express it. There surely must follow in that developing life a sensitivity to the beauty of holiness and a desire to express it.

To have been put in touch, at an early age, with the means of grace is to have received a splendid benediction.

The Soul Restored

Jesus gave a very serious warning to those who sought to 'gain the whole world' at the cost of their souls. Deep down, we know he was right. Erasmus, the Dutch scholar, certainly saw the danger: 'The supreme disaster,' he wrote, 'is the death of the soul.' We would be wise to heed these warnings because we are living in soul-destroying times.

Terrorist bombs do not only bring bereavement, injuries, damage to property and public chaos. They strike at the heart of crucial peace processes. They are, therefore, soul-destroying.

It is not easy today to cultivate the grace of 'whole-souled loveliness'*. So many factors are working against it – the pressures from materialism and secularism, the cult of possessions, the competitive ruthlessness of the acquisitive society, the outrageous financial values put on so-called celebrities in sport and entertainment, sleaze in public life, inequality of opportunity, unemployment and the threat of redundancy. How difficult it is to maintain and develop the spiritual life in face of such soul-destroying forces!

The darkness, the Bible tells us, cannot extinguish the light. For that we thank God. There is, after all, so much that is glorious in his creation, so much in the arts that is inspiring, so much to be admired in truly loving relationships. Add then the conviction that divine grace can make all things new, and hope really does 'spring eternal'. The cultivation of the spiritual dimension is a primary obligation in the religious

* See the next Meditation, Number 61, for the source of this phrase.

life. 'As to the spiritual direction of my soul,' writes Simone Weil, 'I think that God himself has taken it in hand from the start and still looks after it.' God gives us the means of grace to help us restore our souls.

The Lenten pilgrimage provides an opportunity to do just that. The 'interior disturbance' which, according to Jean-Pierre de Caussade, 'renders the soul incapable of applying itself to devotional exercises,' will be alleviated in the company of Jesus whose peace the world cannot give – or take away. The 'guilt of dust and sin', which George Herbert confesses 'draws back the soul', will be forgiven in the company of him whose grace is sufficient for us. The fear that is soul-destroying will be cast out in the company of him who is perfect love.

Enfolded in love, we journey through Lent, ready surely to say with the Psalmist: 'Unto thee, O Lord, do I lift my soul.'

The Grace of Suffering

Lent is an invitation to a pilgrimage. It is a personal journey rehearsing the life of Jesus, a preparatory season that culminates in the wonder of Easter. It offers each pilgrim the opportunity to reflect on Jesus's vocation and ours, his living and ours, his dying and ours. It is a time to recall his perfect life, beyond our attainment but still the model we need to reflect on our failures, while held in that 'love divine, all loves excelling'; to make up lost ground, aware that sanctification develops not as an act of will but by enabling grace. Lent is no 'weary pilgrimage' but a time for growth. However useful it may be to 'give up' something for Lent, the real value is in 'taking in': those who ask and seek will find power through prayer. Lent is, above all, a time for forgiveness and reconciliation, consciously expressed in the ancient practice of receiving back into communion true penitents. With the emphasis on its positive power, Lent is a rewarding experience.

A blessing that comes from the Outer Hebrides speaks to the value of Lent: 'We ask that you shall be blessed with a seven-fold blessing: the grace of form, the grace of goodness, the grace of suffering, the grace of wisdom, the grace of true words, the grace of trust, the grace of whole-souled loveliness.' Whole-souled loveliness! But how can we, as we struggle against the ways of the world, its competitive ruthlessness and its rampant materialism, find that 'whole-souled' quality?

The way of the cross is a road that, for Jesus, runs through suffering. But can suffering be a 'grace' at all? When callous terrorists plant bombs in public places and bring about wounds, death and grief; when illness is added to illness, and bereavement to bereavement, in families we know; when the faces of the starving fill the screens of our television sets and the refugees wander to arid places seeking escape from war, terror and death, how can we speak of the grace of suffering? And yet there is, in the dreadful suffering of Calvary, the graciousness of love, expressed in a prayer for forgiveness for those who, in crucifying him, 'know not what they do' and a promise of paradise for a penitential thief. I find that love somehow reflected in the attitude of those to whom I minister who suffer appallingly from illness, pain, desolation and darkness. How can it be? And yet there comes that acknowledgement of blessing received through suffering and, shining through it, the radiance which reflects whole-souled loveliness.

There is indeed a graciousness around that place of suffering called Calvary. 'The women and the beloved disciple,' writes Tina Beattie in *Rediscovering Mary* (Burns Oates / Dove, 1995), 'stand at the foot of the cross as those righteous ones that keep watch and do not fall asleep, as those who discern the mystery of God's presence in the midst of his most profound absence, as those who represent the possibility of keeping love alive in the depths of hatred and despair.' Suffering sometimes seems to beget grace. It is a mystery indeed.

The Quiet Presence

'There was standing the sorrowing Mother, beside the cross weeping while her Son hung on it.' The thirteenth century hymn, *Stabat Mater dolorosa*, attributed to Jacopone da Todi, plaintively conveys the pain of history's most revered mother as she shares the suffering of her son. It is the pain that every mother – and father – knows who loses a child through death, however it comes. It is heart-breaking. Somewhere, today, someone is going through that pain – waiting, watching, worrying, weeping. Yet, so often, as supremely in Mary, it is borne with dignity.

It is natural to think of Mary on Mothering Sunday. However varied may be the ways in which she is acknowledged in different branches of the church, Mary was, in Jesus's life and death, the quiet presence. She was always there, saying little, giving much.

Mary proclaims her relationship with God through the Magnificat. Faced with an unbelievable proposition by the angelic messenger, her humble, glorious response was 'Yes'. Her words: 'Be it unto me according to thy word' constitute an act of obedience and faith. She gives the 'Yes' that is essential – as it is in prayer, the sacraments and healing – for God to effect a miracle. This is surely the most crucial 'Yes' the world has heard. It makes the Incarnation possible. Elizabeth, her cousin, exclaimed in admiration: 'Blessed are you among women!' How right she was!

The obviously profound relationship between Jesus and Mary was one that she had to learn. So much about her son was unusual – the things he said and did, the way people spoke of him, the expectations he created. As experience succeeded experience, Mary showed her profound sensitivity as (according to St Luke) she 'kept all these things and pondered them in her heart'. She was puzzled but open, instinctively aware if unable to comprehend. The 'devout and just' Simeon, waiting for 'the consolation of Israel', knew that, with her child, that 'consolation' had come. Anna, the prophetess, confirmed it. Confused parents, understandably concerned that their boy was missing in Jerusalem, were (as it must have felt) rebuked by the twelve-year-old Jesus: 'Do you not know that I must be about my Father's business?' Puzzled servants are told by Mary to 'do as he says', and water is turned into wine. At Calvary, Mary was there, the quiet presence, weeping as any other mother would in such awful circumstances, but believing. Jesus's words from the cross show the nature of his relationship with his mother as he commits her to the care, in a mother and son relationship, of 'the disciple whom Jesus loved'.

Beyond the cross, the quiet presence continued. As the disciples gathered in an upper room for prayer, women were present too, and among them, specifically mentioned, is 'Mary, the mother of Jesus'.

'Mary, at the foot of the Cross,' writes Tina Beattie,[*] 'represents the hope of those who continue to believe, even when there is nothing left in heaven and on earth to make sense of their faith.... In her heart she keeps God alive although he is absent from all awareness and reason.'

Let Mary's quiet presence be with you on this Mothering Sunday.

[*] *Rediscovering Mary* (Burns and Oates / Dove, 1995).

A Good Mother

'God could not be everywhere and therefore he made mothers.' So runs a Jewish proverb, happily to be recalled on Mothering Sunday. Motherhood at its best reflects the divine goodness.

The significance of Mary, the mother of Jesus, varies in different branches of the Church, but, whatever attributes are accorded to her across the Christian family, all would surely agree that she is, in the language of today, a superb role model. The hymn of praise known as the *Magnificat*, which she uttered on learning of her unique place in God's purpose, testifies to her innate humility while her spiritual sensitivity is beautifully summed up in her reaction to the events surrounding the Nativity: 'Mary kept all these things and pondered them in her heart.' 'Highly favoured' she was, 'blessed among women,' she was told. She is honoured today for her purity and spirituality by so many. To give thanks for the goodness of Mary is indeed an appropriate way of marking Mothering Sunday.

Goodness is, essentially, the expression of 'God-ness'. If God is love, then at the heart of goodness is love. Such goodness is not something to which we can attain. It evolves within us through the miracle of grace.

As is the case with so much in the spiritual life, the more we try to achieve goodness, the less attainable it becomes. It is, in fact, not an achievement at all. It is a product of the active presence of the Holy Spirit, a fruit in the harvest of the Spirit. If it manifests itself in an individual life, that is evidence of, in New Testament terminology, life 'in Christ'.

Goodness flows from the 'Christ within'. It was said by those who heard the disciples preaching and saw their miracle of healing that 'they took knowledge of them that they had been with Jesus'. In other words, their goodness showed. Such goodness is more visible to others than it is to ourselves. We influence the world most when we are unaware of the goodness we have been given.

This truth lies at the heart of our belief in 'justification by faith alone'. Goodness is not the merit we create in order to claim the divine approval. It is that which develops within us, in the process of sanctification, through 'amazing grace'. If goodness is seen by others to be part of our contribution to the world, the credit for it is not ours. It is due to, as Thomas Binney's hymn says, 'the Holy Spirit's energies'. That makes the possession of goodness, as Mary made clear, a matter for profound humility.

Among the many blessings Jesus brought when 'the Word was made flesh and dwelt among us', was his shining goodness. The rich young ruler recognised this and was moved to address Jesus as 'Good Master'. Jesus felt it right to divert such sincere admiration away from himself, saying: 'Why do you call *me* good? There is only one that is good, and that is God.' The point is understood, but the young man whom Jesus so admired for his honesty was only putting into words the impact of Jesus on those who met him.

As Mothering Sunday comes again, it is right to suggest that some of the Lord's goodness was, surely, the result of his having a good and wonderful mother.

Let there be Light!

Seldom can the threat of impending darkness have been proclaimed as clearly as in the words of Lord Grey of Falloden with the First World War approaching. 'The lamps are going out all over Europe,' he said. 'We shall not see them lit again in our lifetime.' He died in 1933, the year Adolf Hitler became Chancellor of the Third Reich. Darkness would come again. There are times when darkness feel very dense.

Such a time is recalled when Passion Week, the week from Passion Sunday to Palm Sunday, is followed in Holy Week as a journey with Jesus towards Calvary and crucifixion. Matthew, Mark and Luke unite to record the fact that as Jesus's life moved to its close 'there was darkness over all the land from the sixth until the ninth hour.' It was 'gross darkness', significantly symbolic, silently overwhelming. Such darkness descended on the people of Dunblane in a few moments of madness.

The Bible associates darkness with wickedness, sin and suffering. The crucifixion was all of these – the murder of the innocent one who 'hung and suffered there'. Yet the cross is the focus of the glorious paradox that throbs at the heart of faith. Its 'genesis' reaches back to the creation story: 'Darkness was on the face of the deep,' it says, but goes on 'Then the Spirit of God moved on the face of the waters. And God said "Let there be light". And there was light.' Perhaps the paradox is presented most pointedly when we read in Exodus that Moses 'drew near to the darkness *where God was*'. God did not will the murder of the children of Dunblane and their teacher, said the minister of Dunblane

Cathedral, Colin McIntosh, to the parents and people of Dunblane; it is rather that, in those awful moments of darkness, 'God's heart was the first to break'. God is in the darkness. God shares our pain. Somehow in the heart of the darkness of Dunblane, a light began to show. 'The darkness and the light are both alike to thee,' cries the Psalmist exuberantly.

> Aye on the shores of darkness, there is light,
> And precipices show untrodden green,
> There is a budding morrow in midnight ...
>
> — John Keats, *To Homer*

Jesus presented himself as the light of the world, a light which, St John tells us, 'shines in the darkness and the darkness has never extinguished it'(William Barclay's translation). The corollary is unavoidable. Disciples, then and now, must be 'as their Master' and 'let their lights so shine ...' that God is glorified thereby.

Let the words of a child sum up the call of Jesus to his followers. They come from the young Robert Louis Stevenson who, waiting for his supper and looking out on the Edinburgh street in which he lived, was watching the old-fashioned lamplighter on his rounds, lighting each city light. His nurse called him to his meal, but the young Robert refused to take his gaze away from the lamplighter. 'Look, look,' he cried, his face pressed against the window pane, 'there's a man out there punching holes in the darkness.'

So must we all.

The Cords of Love

Robert C. Roberts tells of a lady who was deeply disappointed with most of the literature on spirituality that she found in Christian bookshops. 'It is a little like a down pillow,' she said. 'If you are sleepy, it may be just what you need, but if you want something to stand on, to enable a higher reach, it "squooshes" down too easily. You need something firmer....' She then tried academic theology, and took an adult education course in religion. 'There is intellectual firmness often,' she said, but added, again with disappointment, 'but what can be reached by standing here is not food for the spirit. The stool is strong enough – but I opened a cupboard looking for food and found only various tools and games.'*

It is a sad story for, after all, it is the main purpose of religion to minister to the spirit; that is, in George Steiner's striking phrase, 'to nudge (people) into the neighbourhood of the transcendent'.† There is a gap that needs to be filled and a deep need that must be met, and one of the ways to spiritual sustenance is surely through the Lenten pilgrimage when we journey with Jesus, in reflection, towards Calvary and on to the Garden of the Resurrection. As we take that journey in imagination and memory, we grow into a greater awareness of the divine presence.

If the study of the Master and his ways is the training course for the pupil, let the disciple watch Jesus as he responds to people in need with words and compassionate

* From *Spirituality and Human Emotion* by Robert C. Roberts (Eerdman's / Paternoster Press, 1982).
† Quoted by Stewart Todd in *Theology in Scotland*, Spring 1996.

actions; as he explains and interprets 'the signs of the times'; as he meets hostility with the silence of dignity. After all, is it not recorded that, faced by his accusers, 'Jesus answered them nothing'?

When Jesus entered Jerusalem, a king riding on an ass, 'all the city was moved'. What a complex of emotions he stirred up! There were the happy hosannas and waving palms that we recall each Palm Sunday. There were the Pharisees, sullenly complaining about the disciples' exuberance. There would be, soon, the crowd calling for Barabbas's freedom and Jesus's crucifixion. And still to be faced was the spiritual agony of Gethsemane, the betrayal and denial by two of his disciples, and the physical agony of the cross. And yet he forgave his murderers who 'know not what they do', promised paradise to a penitent thief and committed his mother, Mary, into the safe keeping of the disciple he loved. All this was done though he was despised and rejected, a man of sorrows who 'hung and suffered there'. What manner of man, indeed, is this?

To be, in imagination and awareness, in the company of Jesus as Holy Week unfolds is surely indeed to be nudged into the neighbourhood of the transcendent, to be sanctified by such a demonstration of the divine love.

Let Holy Week bring benediction through feeling the blessing of such amazing grace. How rightly he said that if he were to be 'lifted up from the earth', he would draw everyone to him. He does it with 'the cords of love'.

A Time to Dance

Easter Day is a day not for argument but for affirmation, not for discussion but for dance. It is the triumphant end of the Lenten pilgrimage with Jesus. It is the beginning of his resurrection life.

Recording the fact that Jesus was 'crucified under Pontius Pilate', the Nicene Creed bears witness to the reality of thorns, wood, nails and pain. It is a fact of history that Jesus was 'crucified, died and buried'. Then, however, comes the leap from historic fact to personal conviction. The evidence for the resurrection of Jesus is persuasive in its intensity, but it is the evidence of faith, not logic. As such, it does indeed bear the ring of truth. We have, however, moved into what St Paul calls 'the knowledge which is beyond knowledge' (Ephesians 3:19, *New English Bible*); to a level which goes beyond rational understanding. It is a level of spiritual awareness in which miracles, that is wonder-full things, become possible.

Pilgrims on the Lenten way will have drawn spiritual strength from their journey with Jesus to Calvary's hill, but some will find the next step, where the creeds say that 'he rose again', difficult for it involves not intellect but intuition, not reason but revelation. Peter's confession of his Lord, Jesus points out, is of that latter nature. For Peter to affirm 'Thou art the Son of the living God' could not be a response to 'flesh and blood', but could only come as a revelation 'from my Father which is in heaven'. The disciple, Thomas, could not believe in Jesus's resurrection without proof. Given the evidence, he could exclaim: 'My Lord and my God!'

Significantly, Jesus told him, it involved an act of faith: 'Blessed are they who have not seen, yet have believed.' It is not the logic of events but inner conviction which compels belief in the resurrection. Under the influence of the Holy Spirit, there comes welling up from the inner being a sense of the things one must surely believe.

Many today have to wrestle hard with the paradox which the creeds present, namely that Jesus was, as the Nicene Creed puts it, 'truly human' but at the same time 'true God of true God'. The search for new language, new concepts, new metaphors that will help them to hold these two truths together, will go on, for they are fundamental to Christian faith. 'The Word became flesh and dwelt among us,' so eucharistic devotion will gratefully acknowledge 'the Lamb of God who takest away the sin of the world'. To them Jesus says: 'I am the resurrection and the life.' This is the victory.

'Jesus's resurrection makes it impossible for man's story to end in chaos,' writes Carlo Carretto (in *The Desert in the City*). 'It has to move inexorably towards the light, towards life, towards love'. Or, as my friend Sydney Carter puts it enthusiastically in his famous 'Lord of the Dance', 'They buried my body and they thought I'd gone, but I am the dance and the dance goes on.'

Easter Day is, indeed, not a time for discussion. It is a time to dance.

Resurrection

Jesus instructed his disciples to preach the Gospel, heal the sick *and* 'raise the dead'. The first two exhortations are taken seriously, but boundaries of credulity and of faith are indeed reached when the resurrection of the dead is contemplated. Though some evangelists, particularly of an African background, claim such extraordinary miracles, the possibility of raising the dead goes beyond even the most fervent expectations of faith-full people. While Jesus did carry out such a miracle in the case of Lazarus, we are in a realm in which the disciple just cannot be 'as the Master'. Raising the dead just does not happen today. There was however an occasion some months ago when the word 'resurrection' came into the context of healing ministry.

We were offering thanksgiving for the success of an operation to a lady to relieve excruciating long-term pain and to improve her walking. She is someone of great faith and life-long dedication. One respected surgeon had felt it essential to decline to operate as the risk to life was much too great. There came into the situation a year or two further on another surgeon of reputation and calibre who reconsidered the whole problem. To avoid surgery would leave this lady with perpetual pain and deteriorating movement. He put the crucial question to the patient: 'Are you ready to have this life-or-death operation?' It was no rhetorical question. The possibility of death was very real. 'I shall have to go and pray about it,' she said. 'Yes,' said the surgeon, 'and when you do, pray for the two guys who have got to carry it out!' The long, complicated and extremely tricky operation took place. The patient very nearly died. Giving thanks in our service and in her presence, I found myself talking about a rising from the dead, a resurrection. She truly had new life.

New life is the theme of Easter Day. There are many who believe implicitly in the resurrection of Jesus as scripture records it. There are those who, although they can only interpret the events of the first Easter metaphorically or mythologically, believe in a 'true resurrection'. All share the wonder of the story about new life in Jesus. At the heart of the Christian faith there is the promise of life instead of death, strength in place of weakness, hope in place of despair, victory in place of defeat.

Easter Day is a day held in honour of the gift of new life. Mary Magdalene knew it in the garden of the resurrection when she turned, changed direction, to meet the risen Lord. The disciples knew it when, having contemplated an empty tomb, they received the power of the risen Lord at the first Pentecost. The church knows it as it reflects on the miracles of grace that have brought new life to myriads of people down the years. Each one of us knows it when, in Easter adoration, we say with Thomas: 'My Lord and my God'.

The powers of death have done their worst.
But Christ their legions hath dispersed;
Let shouts of joy outburst –
  Alleluia!

A World 'Smudged'

Gerard Manley Hopkins, in his poem 'God's Grandeur', speaks of a world that is 'seared with trade; bleared, smeared with toil, a world which wears man's smudge and shares man's smell'. Yet, for Hopkins, there is hope. 'Nature is never spent: there lives the dearest freshness deep down things.' And the ground of hope?

> Because the Holy Ghost over the bent
> World broods with warm breast and ah!
>   bright wings

A recent survey among professional people demonstrated the unease so prevalent today. Fears, anxieties and stress were found to be widespread. Personal and family insecurity was rife because of the dread of unemployment. A large number of those questioned could not rule out the possibility of redundancy within a year. But there was a greater threat – inner insecurity. Was society itself 'breaking up'? Did the future offer any hope of quality of life? The world was perceived as one which glamorises the trivial and minimises the spiritual; as one which abounds in goods but not in grace; a world where corruption is cutting confidence, where violence and perversion make their presence felt; a world 'smudged' indeed. But people with faith cannot abandon hope, for it is over this 'bent' world that the brooding Spirit moves, with warmth, to heal and to save.

There are many, too, who feel disconsolate over the institution 'church'. Insiders grieve that years of enthusiasm, commitment and prayer yield only discouraging results.

Outsiders dismiss the church as irrelevant. Yet here there is a paradox that will stimulate and excite those able to see the presence of the brooding spirit in it. There are many signs that the desire for the spiritual dimension is alive and strong, especially among younger people. It is a quest which, sadly, so often by-passes the 'official' church, but the indicators provide evidence of its reality – the immense interest in contemplation and especially meditation; the large number of people who fill retreat houses, healing homes and centres for prayer; the demand for spiritual direction. Many seek to make 'the inner journey' through contact with eastern religion, the pursuit of esoteric philosophies and even curious cults. Not all these roads are safe (some forms of meditation, for example, carry risks), but these indicators point to the need for 'deep calling to deep', the depth of human need crying out for a ministry to those deep down things.

The primary task of the church is to proclaim and demonstrate the wonder of life in the Spirit, to offer the resources of the faith to the needy and to present the opportunity of 'new life'. It is surely not an accident that the most obviously growing churches are those expressing pentecostal fervour and offering charismatic renewal, which seem to meet the need for a living, loving fellowship concerned with spiritual needs known and unknown.

In an age of overwhelming suffering, it is essential that the ministry of Jesus to the whole person – physical, mental, emotional and spiritual – be fully recovered. Jesus reaches deep down things. Is it not the 'brooding, warm spirit' that is pressing on the churches the importance, as a normal part of its witness, of the healing ministry?

The Encourager

Andrew was not the most publicly prominent of the twelve apostles. There are, in fact, few references to him in the Gospel records. That reticence may reflect his nature – I see him as a rather shy, introverted man, in contrast to his 'front of stage' brother, Peter, who was extrovert and outspoken (often to his cost, but glorious in his confession of Christ). Andrew's presence may be muted, but he was important to the apostolic band and represents so much that is important for the church today.

Andrew fulfilled the primary command of Jesus to 'preach the gospel'; he became in particular the evangelist to Scythia. In that he took his leader's instructions seriously, he was faithful to that primary means of communication, the proclamation of the word. Andrew's witness to that function has certainly been taken seriously by the church of the nation of which he became patron saint, Scotland. The importance laid on preaching has been recognised in some traditions by the layout of the church buildings: the pulpit has been given the dominant central place with extensive seating provided for the many who would come to hear the gospel. That physical arrangement has sometimes led to a diminished presence for 'the table of the Lord', but it does remind us that – unfashionable as it may presently be – the exposition of the word remains a priority for the Church.

Andrew was not (as Peter, James and John were) present at the great spiritual experiences of the Transfiguration of Jesus and his agony in Gethsemane, but that he was one of the inner circle of the disciples seems to be implied by the reference in Mark to his being the fourth of the disciples who spoke 'privately' to Jesus about coming events. If that is so, he was clearly close to Jesus, something that must surely have contributed to his character and personality. That intimacy helped him to bring others to Jesus. It is of the essence of the Church's work to follow that example and bring individual people into a close relationship with Christ.

Andrew was an encourager. His role in the apostolic band seems to have been a facilitating one, as two incidents show. First, we are told that Greeks came to Philip saying: 'Sir, we would see Jesus.' To whom does Philip turn to make that meeting possible? To Andrew, of course. The other reference is to the call of Andrew to be a disciple. He willingly responds, but first calls his brother, Simon (Peter). 'And he brought him to Jesus.'

To make it possible for human beings with needs to see, to meet and to understand Jesus is – as it was for St Andrew – the essential purpose of the church. Academic theology has, of course, its place but it is not doctrinaire discussion or the intricacies of inter-church relations that bring salvation. It is those things for which such as St Andrew so simply yet profoundly stands that lead to life. To bring 'good news', to nurture a relationship with Christ, to offer a ministry of encouragement – these are the first responsibilities of the Church, now and always.

Part V

The Healing Ministry

Firm Foundations

Some of the most important insights into healing ministry come not from the Gospel records of the miracles of Jesus but from the report of a healing miracle effected by the disciples. It is, significantly, the doctor among the evangelists who tells us of the miracle of the lame man healed by Peter 'in the name of Jesus Christ of Nazareth', and also of the public consequences of that action.

The miracle is described in Acts 3, and the consequences of it in Acts 4. Within that latter chapter are four matters on which reflection will usefully be made.

First to be noticed is the number of times the word 'boldness' comes into the story. The authorities saw their boldness, the disciples' prayer was that they should 'speak the word with boldness', and Luke's report is that they did 'speak the word with boldness'. This fearlessness (to use William Barclay's translation of the same word) is necessary if the gospel is to be proclaimed today. To speak of signs, wonders and the possibility of healing miracles to a scientifically conditioned and materialistic world requires boldness; not the boldness of arrogance but the fearlessness of conviction. To be involved in healing ministry and indeed true proclamation 'in Jesus's name' today requires such boldness.

Secondly, the ministry the disciples were trying to effect was, as they testified, the work of the Holy Spirit. And so must all such ministry be. Those who feel called to the Christian ministry of healing do not speak of themselves as 'healers' as some others do. It is the risen Christ who is the agent of miracle. He seeks those who will be channels for his

164

healing power but the power, like the glory, belongs to him alone.

Thirdly, look at the reference made to the apostles by those who observed them. 'They took knowledge of them that they had been with Jesus.' The disciples would almost certainly be surprised to realise that they had – by what they did and said, by what they were – proclaimed their allegiance. That message had certainly come through. All who seek to serve as disciples should have a similar effect. If they do, it will be demonstrated by the attitudes they show. These is no place for arrogance in those who engage in the ministry of healing, only humility. To have such an influence without realising it is discipleship indeed.

Fourthly, and most significantly of all, the report reveals how totally the disciples had understood the message of their leader. 'Now, Lord,' they prayed, 'grant unto thy servants that with all boldness they may speak thy word, by stretching out thine hand to heal.' Miracles, signs and wonders are the symbols, signs and seals of the truth of the gospel.

Jesus, in sending out the disciples, said: 'Preach the Gospel, heal the sick.' Preaching and healing are but two sides of the same coin, the miracles of healing being demonstrations in action of the compassion the gospel proclaims. Preaching and healing together constitute the firm foundations of the faith.

Holy Harmony

Health is 'a state of complete physical, mental and social well-being and not merely the absence of disease or infirmity'. This definition of health, offered by the World Health Organisation in 1948, remains a satisfactory one. Those with a religious background may feel, however, that it is less than an ideal definition because of its lack of reference to a spiritual component.

The Old Testament always sees good health as including a happy relationship with God. The New Testament makes use of several words in this context. There is, for example, the Greek word for peace (*eirene*), the one that comes nearest to that almost indefinable but extraordinarily expressive Hebrew word, *shalom*. Then there is the word *teleios* meaning 'maturity' and, in the New Testament sense, 'perfection'. Another word is *soteria* of which the root meaning is 'safe and sound'. In Greek translations of the Old Testament, it came to mean deliverance (for example the deliverance of the children of Israel at the Red Sea) and further developed its meaning in the New Testament as the word for 'spiritual safety', namely salvation. That association between health and salvation is interesting.

If there is any definition of health in the New Testament, Paul's first letter to the Thessalonians (5:23, *New English Bible*) provides it: 'May God himself, the God of peace, make you holy in every part and keep you sound in spirit, soul and body, without fault when our Lord Jesus Christ comes.' Wholeness and holiness come close together in this benediction.

Are there any contemporary concepts or images that help us further to define the meaning of health? There are two possibilities, of which the first is *balance*.

Those who seek healing are usually yearning for physical restoration. There is nothing wrong in that. The majority of Jesus's healing miracles involved physical healing. That acknowledged, it is essential to recognise that we are not just bodies. We have also mental, emotional and spiritual aspects to our being. Conscious as we are today of psychosomatic factors in illness, we can see the interdependence between those four aspects. Dis-ease in our emotional or spiritual life may well contribute to disease in our bodies. To see health therefore as the achievement of balance in the inter-relationship of the physical, mental, emotional and spiritual aspects of our being may well point us towards a significant understanding of what good health means.

The other image which may be of help is *harmony*, 'the pleasing interaction or an appropriate combination of the elements in a whole'. When every aspect of our being is, through discipline and grace, in harmony, we must be on the way to health and wholeness. And, if wholeness and holiness are indeed close in meaning, we can helpfully and happily describe good health as 'holy harmony'.

By Word and Touch

The teaching of Jesus has had an immeasurable impact on the life of the world. The wonder of his wisdom and insight has fascinated people far beyond the confines of the Church. And rightly so. He brought together a profound spirituality that leads the pilgrim into the realm of 'the eternal' and yet no teacher was more practical and down-to-earth than he was.

For some, Jesus's healing ministry is even more fascinating than his teaching ministry. It certainly must have intrigued St Luke, a physician, as much as it impressed him. There are many miracles of healing recorded in Luke's Gospel. Equally interesting is the variety Jesus showed in his approach to healing. Sometimes he healed by word alone, sometimes by touch, sometimes by word *and* touch.

When Jesus healed by word alone, the key element seemed to be his authority. This was especially so in his casting out of demons. He never laid hands on the demon-possessed. Cases in which he used words of command, usually addressed to the demon, are those of the demoniac in the synagogue, the Gadarene demoniac and an epileptic boy who had 'a foul spirit'.

What is impressive in all these cases is the *authority* of his words. Whether Jesus is casting out demons or carrying out physical healings (as in one case of a paralysed man), he is issuing orders with the power of the kingdom as the background to what he is doing. This is the same in the other category of miracles, attested by word alone, the raising of the dead. To Lazarus he said: 'Lazarus, come out.' The dead cannot hear commands, but the issuing of the order is in terms of the authority and power which Jesus says comes from the Father.

If authority is the key concept in healing by word alone, compassion is at the heart of healing by touch alone. The ministry of touch is expressed as laying on of hands (as in the case of the man with dropsy, or that of Malchus whose ear was cut off by Peter – according to John's Gospel) and is always an act of compassion. So far as a combination of word *and* touch is concerned, authority and compassion are welded together. In the case of Peter's mother-in-law, he 'rebuked the fever' and 'he touched her hand'.

So are word and/or touch essential in healing? No, for on three occasions certainly Jesus healed people at a distance from him. There was, for example, the Roman centurion who pleaded with Jesus for his servant. Jesus immediately offered to go and heal him. The centurion however appealed to Jesus whom he saw as a man in authority. 'Just speak the word only, and my servant shall be healed,' he said. He was.

What a marvellously moving statement of belief in the authority and compassion of Jesus! No wonder he commented that he had not found 'so great faith, no, not in Israel'.

Absent Healing

One of the most illuminating comments Jesus made in relation to his work of healing was his response to the woman
who, famously, 'touched the hem of his garment' in the hope
of a cure for her uterine haemorrhage, a condition from
which she had suffered for twelve years. Clearly the woman
believed that any contact with Jesus, be it only the tassel of his
cloak, constituted the possibility of cure. The extraordinary
aspect of the incident was the awareness that Jesus had of her
touch. After all, he was surrounded by a crowd of people
pressing in upon him, yet he sensed that he had been touched
by someone in particular need. 'Who touched my clothes?' he
asked. Helpfully he gave the reason for his awareness of what
had happened. He knew 'in himself that power had gone out
of him'.

This is a clear indication that Jesus believed power was in
some way transmitted in the act of healing where faith was
present. 'Your faith has made you whole.' This surely has
implications for those called to the healing ministry and to
minister 'in his name'. The laying on of hands is not only a
symbolic act, but the means whereby the power of the risen
Lord, present in this ministry, is conveyed to those who, in
faith, seek it. Laying on of hands is more than a liturgical
symbol. It is an act of transformation; an act which testifies
not to the healing power of the minister involved, but testifies
to the eternal Christ at work in the world where those who
believe in him minister 'in his name'.

Sometimes Jesus uses one method in healing, sometimes
another. It is however clear that none of these methods – for

example, words, touch, saliva – was essential for the transmission of divine power to those who needed it, for there were occasions when he healed people who were not in his presence at all. Three examples come to mind. There was John's report of the healing of the nobleman's son. There was Mark's story of the Syrophoenician woman who pleaded for her daughter's cure. There was the centurion's servant referred to in St Matthew's Gospel. Word, touch, word *and* touch, were not essential components in healing. It took place too when there was no contact at all. There is then a place for what some would call 'absent healing' in the ministry of the Church. It may be that someone brings another's need to the altar rail as the centurion brought his servant's need to Jesus. Intercession specifically focussed and supported by group prayer is a vital part of healing ministry. What matters is not technique or method, word, touch, saliva, essential presence or accepted absence. The great and glorious truth is that Jesus heals today; that 'his touch has not lost its ancient power'; that, while God offers healing through the gifts of creation – medicine, psychotherapy, music, healing relationship and some (but not all) of the complementary therapies – there is available to all the transmission of power in response to prayer, pleading and faith. The result is changed lives. Those in need are made more whole.

Healing Music

'Music alone with sudden charms can bind the wandering sense, and calm the troubled mind.' So wrote William Congreve, who died in 1729, but many centuries before that a demented king of Israel sensed the truth of that claim. When 'an evil spirit tormented him', King Saul's attendants suggested that he ask for 'someone who can play on the harp' and 'you will feel better'. One of the servants specifically suggested David, 'a son of Jesse of Bethlehem who knows how to play the harp ... and the Lord is with him'. Then relief would come to Saul, he would feel better and 'the evil spirit would leave him'. The story (in 1 Samuel 16, *New International Version*) is an intriguing testimony to the healing power of music.

When the remarkable Healing and Counselling Centre in the crypt of St Marylebone Parish Church in London was envisaged and effected by the then Rector, Christopher Hamel Cooke, the grand vision was of an agency incorporating four disciplines that would, under one roof, minister to the needs that people brought, be they physical, mental, emotional or spiritual. The four agencies were (i) that church's healing and counselling ministry; (ii) a National Health Service practice; (iii) healing organisations and (iv) a music therapy unit. In that plan, the place of music in healing was significantly recognised. Unfortunately that fourth element had, for practical reasons, to cease but the concept incarnated in that centre proclaimed the place of church, medicine, healing organisations and music therapy in co-operative ministry to wholeness.

The spoken word and the written word will continue to be crucial in the proclamation of the gospel. In healing the sick – so linked with preaching in Jesus's instructions to the disciples – pastoral care, counselling, psychotherapy, spiritual direction, etc., will play their part, as will healing relationships, for God uses people to help people in ministering to emotional and spiritual dis-ease. But all who are involved in healing ministry constantly agonise over the difficulties which are encountered when mental limitation makes words of little use and customary pastoral practices largely irrelevant. What a healing gift music can be in that situation. Dr Glen Wilson, a distinguished music therapist, puts it clearly: 'Music plugs more directly into feelings than words. Words have to go through intermediate stages for construction, such as dealing with pictures and synthesising memory. Music goes straight in.' The results are often dramatic.

Beethoven's capacity to compose while profoundly deaf, Katharine Hadley notes, 'is well documented, but he also used it to comfort himself. While he was dying, he chose one piece, the String Quartet in B flat, opus 130 (Cavatina), perhaps the music he wanted the world to recognise as his personal signature tune. He read the score repeatedly, and wrote: "I leave my music to heal the world".'*

The music that heals is surely one of God's gracious gifts to the world.

* * *

* An article on 'Music on the Mind' was published in *Classic FM* magazine in May 1996.

Credo

Commitment to a belief depends on two factors. The first is the testimony of personal experience, the second the confirmation of that experience by some external authority. The subjective factor, experience, needs objective affirmation. For non-religious people that external confirmation will most likely come from the experience of others, the validity of their similar experience, especially if multiplied by many examples, confirming the authenticity of one's own experience. Religious people will find their external authority in another specific form, depending on their church background. Some will find the authority they need in the tradition of their church with its record of God's grace to people down the ages. Others, especially those like myself in the 'evangelical and reformed' tradition, will test their experience against 'the word of God'.

Such external authority is essential. Human nature is flawed and the flaw extends to all aspects of our being. The problem is what Paul describes as that 'law in our members' expressing itself in his famous statement that when we 'would do good, evil is present with us'. The world of psychoanalysis similarly demonstrates how easily we fall victim to psychological mechanisms that threaten the reliability of our experience. We can rationalise a situation and make ourselves believe that we are taking action for one reason when unconsciously we are doing it for another. We can confuse the will of God with wishful thinking. The imagination can run riot and endanger the reliability of our deductions from experience. To have validity and authority for our beliefs and to feel confidence in them, the subjective and objective factors must come together.

For me, the external authority is that supreme rule of faith and life (as we declare in our ordination vows), the Bible, thus giving biblical authority to our experience. When revelation to ourselves is confirmed by God's revelation to other people in many ages, and authenticated by its inclusion in the canon of Scripture, we stand on solid ground. It is the Holy Spirit at work in history and in our own experience.

The four convictions which for me provide such stability and lead to commitment are the doctrines of providence, forgiveness, salvation and healing. I find my experience of providence compelling and convincing. Looking back on all the failures, successes, dangers, decisions, crises I can see that ultimately all things work together for good in extraordinary ways. I see apparently unconnected events brought into some kind of miraculous juxtaposition in such a way as to move faith forward.

I read the Gospel statements about forgiveness and from my experience know how true they are. I read the theory of what the religious vocabulary calls salvation, or redemption, or new life, or meaning and my deepest intuitions confirm that it is true. I believe in the healing power of the risen Christ. It is on record. But I know it from experience.

This reflection on authority and experience seems to have turned into a personal credo, but it just may encourage others to believe and make their commitment.